Ken Duncum grew up in Rotorua and has been writing for theatre and television for nearly twenty years. He is recognised as one of New Zealand's leading playwrights, with a record three plays in the all-time 'Top 30' list of New Zealand plays (as voted by theatre professionals).

In the 1980s Duncum worked with Rebecca Rodden. Their full-length play, *Jism* (1989) was named Play of the Year by the *Dominion*. Duncum's subsequent work for screen and stage includes the plays *Flipside* (Chapman Tripp Award for Production of the Year 2000), *Waterloo Sunset*, and *Blue Sky Boys* (Best New Zealand Play 1990), as well as scripts for major television shows like *Duggan* and *Coverstory* (Best Script, TV Drama, Film and TV Awards 1997). In September 2001 Duncum was the inaugural recipient of the Michael Hirschfeld Memorial Writing Award, and in 2002 he began as the Michael Hirschfeld Director of Scriptwriting, coordinating the MA in scriptwriting at Victoria University's International Institute of Modern Letters.

Ken Duncum's latest play, *Cherish*, won Best New New Zealand Play at the Chapman Tripp Theatre Awards in 2003 – making it two in a row after *Trick of the Light* won the same award the previous year.

T0159759

Plays 1: Small Towns and Sea

HORSEPLAY

FLIPSIDE

TRICK OF THE LIGHT

KEN DUNCUM

VICTORIA UNIVERSITY PRESS

VICTORIA UNIVERSITY PRESS
Victoria University of Wellington
PO Box 600, Wellington
www.vuw.ac.nz/vup

in association with
THE PLAY PRESS
PO Box 27-436, Wellington
www.playpress.co.nz

In *Horseplay* quotations from
the writings of James K. Baxter are reprinted
with kind permission of Jacquie Baxter

Flipside was adapted with permission from *Capsized*
by James Nalepka and Steven Callahan,
HarperCollins, Auckland, 1992

National Library of New Zealand Cataloguing-in-Publication Data
Duncum, Ken, 1959-
Plays 1 : small towns and sea / Ken Duncum.
(New Zealand playscripts)
ISBN 0-86473-494-8
I. Title. II. Series.
NZ822.3—dc 22

Published with the assistance of a grant from

ARTS COUNCIL OF NEW ZEALAND *TOI AOTEAROA*

Printed by Printlink, Wellington

Contents

Author's Note   7

Horseplay   9

Flipside   85

Trick of the Light   183

Author's Note

These three plays are set either in small New Zealand towns or out on the sea that hits up hard against those small towns. They're plays which stem from New Zealand myths – in the sense of Great Stories which somehow reverberate for us.

Most of our myths are 'true stories' – the saga of the *Rose-Noëlle*, the mystery of the Crewe murders, the larger-than-lives of James K. Baxter and Ronald Hugh Morrieson. They fascinate us because they are us.

'Know your murders, Clare. It's our heritage in this country.'

HORSEPLAY

Introduction

I'd say there are very few real guidelines about creating story and characters – but one that always made a lot of sense to me and which I generally observe is 'Don't write about writers'. With *Horseplay* I completely flouted that advice.

Although living for a time, and now buried, at no great distance from each other, James K. Baxter and Ronald Hugh Morrieson as far as we know did not cross paths. The idea of putting them both in the one room came from the same-but-different nature of their lives: the way they paralleled or reflected each other – and therefore what each could tell us about the other. Also from the biographical detail that perhaps most unites the real men – their deaths within months of each other, one feeling unsung, the other defeated. Or – I wondered – was that too simple? Was there a way of understanding the end of their lives as something more than a dying fall?

The other reason for putting the two men together was a desire on my part to play with language. I was attracted to the way Baxter and Morrieson could and did express themselves poetically – Baxter's poetry of course, Morrieson's intensely colourful and colloquial imagery, the way they both swooped from the sacred to the profane and back again, passing through naturalistic speech only as a comparatively dismal railway station somewhere en route. I wanted to write something with big juicy language. In Baxter and Morrieson I had verbal thoroughbreds more than equal to the task. My challenge was to keep up with them.

Once I had the concept of the meeting, and the year it would take place, the setting took care of itself. I've always liked Hawera, partly for itself – its water tower and Elvis Presley Memorial Record Room – and partly for Morrieson's mythologised town which still overlays the real streets like a transparency. Morrieson going to Jerusalem would have been like him visiting the moon. Baxter staggering into Morrieson's Hawera towards the end of his long and strange journey made sense – it could push him to revisit and reconnect with things he had left behind. Left behind in the old New Zealand which only now survived in pockets like the actual Hawera, or even more so the storied Hawera that Morrieson spins around Baxter in the dead of night.

The actors in the first production of Horseplay at Bats Theatre in Wellington brought a sense of physical panache to match the verbal acrobatics. Every night Duncan Smith as Morrieson sent a bottle of whisky flying along and off the table where it was caught one-handed in mid-air by William Kircher with such verve that the audience would burst into applause.

Two performances of Horseplay stand out in my mind – a one-night stand in Hawera to a full audience many of whom had known Ronald Hugh Morrieson. We were received with warmth and generosity, not the lynching I had feared, and it was a privilege to be able to 'play it back' in the place the story had started. The other memorable night was when James K. Baxter's family came to see the show in Wellington and sat in the front row of Bats, a small venue at the best of times but smaller still when you're playing someone's husband or father right in front of them. Their support and enjoyment of the play was a relief and a boost.

I'm particularly grateful to Jacquie Baxter/J. C. Sturm, whose reaction to the whole idea of the play could have been very different from what it was. I'll never forget sitting in her lounge telling her what I had in mind for her dead husband and reaching the point where he's perched on the top of a door after a failed murder attempt and a botched suicide. To say I had my fingers crossed would be an understatement. Her understanding of what I was trying to do – or preparedness to trust me – was sublime, and her permission to quote Baxter's poetry enabled his voice to be heard more fully in the play.

Someone wrote: the aim of any discussion should not be victory but progress. Baxter and Morrieson are two strong personalities – onstage as in life – but ultimately their meeting moves each one on in his understanding of himself and his separate but similar destiny. That is what I wanted to present with this play – not a competition and certainly no winner. Both men arrive at the same place by different paths. I've walked the dusty road at Jerusalem, beside a slow bend of the Whanganui, and I've stood in the Hawera KFC and looked at the plaque which says Ronald Hugh Morrieson's house stood here. The feeling was the same.

First Performance

Horseplay was first performed at Bats Theatre, Wellington, on
11 November 1994, with the following cast:

RONALD HUGH MORRIESON	Duncan Smith
JAMES K. BAXTER	William Kircher
WILMA	Carol Smith
AUNT	Dinah Priestley

Director	William Walker
Designer	Prunella Wilde
Producer	Duncan Smith
Stage Manager/Technician	Martyn Roberts
Lighting and Sound Design	Alistair Edwards
Publicity	Terry Bloomfield
Set Construction	Keith Tait and Tim Thomas
Graphics	Gregory Millen
Horse built by	Weta Productions

Characters

RONALD HUGH MORRIESON (RON)	– 50
JAMES K. BAXTER (JIM)	– 46
WILMA	– 36
AUNT	– 70s

Setting

Late August, 1972, in the large kitchen of an old family home in Hawera. Clearly where most of the living in the house is done, it has a dining table and chairs, two faded armchairs on a square of carpet in front of a fireplace now containing an electric fire. There are a number of shelves crammed tight with books, and an upright piano, a photo of Morrieson's dead mother on it. A typewriter sits on a side table or desk. There is an internal door leading to the rest of the house. The back door of the house opens into the kitchen. Beyond it are no doubt a porch and washhouse.

Act One

*It is somewhere around midnight. The kitchen is unlit. Moonlight through the window vaguely illuminates the figure of an elderly woman (*Aunt*). In her nightgown she stands beside the piano fingering a few keys and crooning a song to herself. She refills her glass of sweet sherry from the bottle standing on top of the piano, and knocks it back.*

She is suddenly alerted by the headlights and sound of a truck pulling in outside the window. Alarmed, she hurries to close the piano and replace the bottle and glass in a cupboard. As the engine continues to run, a door of the truck slams.

Ron, *off*: Take the wheel, mate! I'll drop the tray! (*There is a clang, followed by a thump like something heavy hitting the ground.*) Keep her ticking over – I'll run the rope round something!

Just as Aunt *escapes unnoticed through the internal door, the back door opens and* Ron Morrieson *enters. He is a big, rounded, bullet-headed man. Aged 50, he still looks powerful, with a build similar to a wrestler, although the ravages of booze and illness become obvious if you observe him for any length of time. He is a chain-smoker and a cigarette dangles from his lip. He takes subsequent pre-rolled cigarettes from a silver cigarette case he carries in his pocket. He wears an old overcoat which he doesn't take off throughout the play. As usual at this time of night he is half cut. In one hand he holds the end of a tow rope. His eyes narrow to slits in his puffy, corpulent face as he glances round speculatively, looking for a strong enough anchor. He threads the rope through some struts supporting the kitchen bench and exits to attach the end to the truck.*

RON, *off*: OK mate. Easy does it. (*The engine revs. The slack in the rope is taken up. The engine noise grows louder as the truck strains.*) Bit more toe!

> *The rope starts to travel through the struts. Something heavy is being dragged towards the house. It bumps up into the porch outside the back door.* MORRIESON *appears outside the door again, signalling instructions.*

Beauty! Reverse up and I'll get the rope off! (*There is a horrible crashing of gears as the driver tries to find reverse. The engine roars. The rope jerks into action as, outside, the truck lurches forward out of control.*) Reverse! Reverse!

> MORRIESON *is forced to jump inside as, attached to the end of the rope, the upside-down hindquarters of a dead horse appear suddenly in the back door. Under the runaway pull of the truck the legs (sticking stiffly up) and rump roughly bump their way through the door, but the distended mid-section causes the horse to jam.*

Whoa, mate! Whoa!

> *Too late. The strain comes squarely on the bench serving as anchor point. Cracking and splintering, it comes apart, the rope twanging, the wreckage being dragged across the room. There is a crash outside as the truck runs full tilt into something solid. The engine revs for a moment then cuts out.*

> *Silence.* MORRIESON *surveys the scene of wreckage.*

That's puckerooed it. (*There is the sound of the truck door opening.* MORRIESON *looks out the window.*) Well you'd be the biggest no-hoper twat a man'd meet in a day's march. (*He sucks his teeth, feeling some discomfort in his guts.*) Come on, mate, let's be having ya. Looks like some serious cogitation and a change of strategy is called for.

The AUNT'*s voice is heard from behind the door.*

AUNT, *off*: Ronald? Ronald, are you there?
RON: Christ!

He springs across the room to block the AUNT *as she opens the door –*

AUNT: Ronald?

– preventing her entering, and screening the scene of destruction from her view.

RON: Yep. Just me, Aunty.
AUNT: I heard a crash.
RON: Yeah, I – dropped a milk bottle. (*It sounded more like the house had taken a direct hit from a grand piano.*) Went off like a bomb. Glass everywhere. Better not come in.
AUNT, *noticing he's nursing his guts*: Are you hurt?
RON, *taking his hand away and straightening*: Nah – right as rain.
AUNT: Oh, Ronnie, not your tummy again.
RON: I told you, never been better. You get off back to bed and I'll clear everything up here.
AUNT, *looking like she's going to say something, but instead*: I put the brush and pan here in the hall cupboard.

She disappears to get them. A dazed-looking BAXTER *appears outside the door or window. Spotting him,* MORRIESON *hisses to gain his attention and furiously waves his arm for him to get back out of sight. This sinks in and* BAXTER, *still dazed, retreats. The* AUNT *returns and passes the brush and pan set through the door to* MORRIESON.

Now promise me you'll be careful, Ronald. You can't give guitar lessons if your fingers are cut.

RON: I will. Night-night, Aunty.

> *She goes.* MORRIESON *closes the door. He shapes up to the wreckage and the wedged horse carcass with the hopelessly inadequate brush and pan, then sighs and drops them. Wincing at the pain in his stomach, he takes a medicine bottle from his pocket, fumbles out a few pills and swallows them – washed down with whisky from a half-full bottle he retrieves from a cupboard. He crosses to the window and impatiently gestures the unseen* BAXTER *inside.*

And bring the grog. A man could die of thirst in here.

> MORRIESON *swigs from the whisky again. There is a scuffle and a clanking at the door.* BAXTER *reappears and passes over some flagons. Shakily clambering over the carcass,* BAXTER *stumbles on the horse and sprawls into the kitchen.*

Keep the bloody noise down! There's an old lady tryna sleep!

> MORRIESON *makes no attempt to moderate his own volume.* BAXTER *gets slowly to his feet and stands – cold, dazed and exhausted.*

> BAXTER *is 46, but looks older. He is in his Jerusalem phase with long hair and beard. He is barefoot, dressed in a grubby secondhand suit and wears a silver cross on rosary beads round his neck. Cadaverous, stooped – with slightly arched shoulders and a heavy head projected forward – he moves with a loose, almost shambling gait. A patch of hair above his forehead is matted with blood. His voice, when it comes, is resonant.*

JIM: Perhaps I should have double-clutched.
RON, *regarding him levelly*: Just one thing puzzles me, mate. Did

you have go to school to be such a prick – or does it just
come natural? You bollocks my house, prang the truck – if
I owned a dog I bet you'd have run the bugger over – and
I don't even know you from Adam! (*He extends his hand.*)
Ron.

JIM, *shaking limply*: Hemi.

> MORRIESON *reacts to the Maori name as if* BAXTER'*s trying
> to put something across him.*

RON: Get away. (*He scrutinises* BAXTER.) Scrape the rubble off a
pew and sit yourself down, mate. Have a peer through the
tawny telescope.

> *He pushes the whisky at* BAXTER, *who just manages to
> keep hold of it. As* MORRIESON *goes in search of glasses,*
> BAXTER *places the bottle on the table and wanders vaguely
> around the room, preoccupied, looking at this and that.*
> MORRIESON *glances at him sharply, a bit concerned, as*
> BAXTER *runs his fingers along the spines of the books in the
> bookcase.*

My aunt used to run a bit of a lending library. Not much
of a reader myself. (*Remembering the typewriter, he quickly
throws something over it to cover it.*) The *Best Bets* is about
my speed. All the characters you could want and a mystery
right to the end.

> BAXTER *is just reaching for a book (* The Scarecrow*) lying
> flat on top of other books on a shelf, when* MORRIESON
> *arrives to cut him off at the pass.*

Hemi, eh? Yeah – now you mention it – can see you've
got a touch of the tar brush. No worries. Half-cut or half-
caste it's all the same to me. (*Brandishing glasses and whisky
bottle,* MORRIESON *backs* BAXTER *into one of the armchairs.
He pours the drinks.*) Where were you coming from when I

picked you up, mate?

JIM: Fleeing Jerusalem.

RON: That explains the Old Testament haircut. No offence but every holy roller I ever met came complete with short back and sides. Except old Clem Bascoe of course – never saw a man like him for being taken by the spirit. Methylated in his case.

You're not on your way to visit old Clem are you? (BAXTER *shakes his head.*) Lucky. Had a bit of trouble old Clem. Did an unwise thing for a metho drinker and took up smoking. Shortly after that he took up bursting into flames.

> BAXTER *shivers, pulling his thin clothes around him.* MORRIESON *gestures at the fireplace.*

Let me get this on for you, mate. (*He turns on the electric fire.*) Gonna be a snorter of a frost I reckon. (MORRIESON *rubs his hands and holds them to the flickering fire.* BAXTER *follows suit with his stiff and frozen hands and feet.*) Corker, eh? Element burnt out a year ago – but the lights are beauty.

> *He drinks, then notices that* BAXTER *hasn't touched his.*

Get that down you, mate. (BAXTER *stares at the glass.*) Better than any heater. Plug a few of those into your belly and we could use your bum as a pop-up toaster.

JIM, *overcoming the temptation*: I don't drink.

> *This is not the way to blend in in Hawera.*

RON: Eh? Why not?

JIM: I'm an alcoholic.

RON: So am I, mate – but I never let it get in the way of my drinking.

JIM, *getting up again restlessly*: What town is this?

RON, *staring at him*: What town? You'd be joking wouldn't you? Take a dekko out the window and what hits you straight in the eye? If it was daylight. Only the finest bloody water tower in the country! (BAXTER *looks blank*.) What town is this? The pearl of South Taranaki! Gateway to the north – of Taranaki. Paris under the mountain! Hawera, mate. (*He pronounces it 'Hara'.*) Hawera.

> MORRIESON *seems lost in reverie.* BAXTER *puts his hand up to his head. It comes away tacky with blood.*

A name to conjure with. (MORRIESON *notices* BAXTER *examining the blood, as if coming to himself.*) That'd be from collecting the dash. When we ran into Trigger over there.

JIM: You picked me up in your truck. I was walking. No, running—

RON: More like crawling when I saw you, mate. Lucky I happened by when I did.

JIM: Running from Te Taipo – the Maori demon. Risen from the urupa beside the middle house at Hiruharama . . . The spirit of death I have seen there before.

RON: I thought you'd carked it when you fell asleep in the truck. I was just rolling a smoke and thinking about swinging by the undertakers soon as I got to town – when I looked up and there was this bloody great gee-gee. (*He smacks his hands together to simulate the collision.*) First horse in orbit.

> BAXTER *just stares distractedly at* MORRIESON, *then heads for the door.*

Hey, where you going? (*He intercepts* BAXTER.) You'll freeze to buggery!

JIM: I won't stop for it, I won't stand still for it, d'ye hear!

RON: Look, mate, no one's going anywhere. For a bloody good reason. It just so happens – (MORRIESON *takes his elbow and indicates the wedged horse.*) – this is no ordinary donkey we've bowled.

JIM: Can't let him catch me, see!

RON: Who?

JIM: Death. Who takes all things. Death of the word. All the chook-scratchings in the ashes. Death of good intentions . . . (BAXTER *is animated by passion.*) But not death of our sins. Eh? Not the death of our failures. Te Taipo won't wrap those up in his fetid coat and take them down into his swamp. We have to bear them, we have to come when we're whistled – each man to be judged – dragging the horse carcass of his life, that no self-respecting vulture would pick at. What kind of bastard is he?

RON: Eh?

JIM: God! To kill a man when he's down.

> *Pause.*

My thanks for the lift.

> BAXTER *turns to go.* MORRIESON *summons all his gravity.*

RON: You talk about death? You must be keen to meet him if you want to step outside that door. (BAXTER *stops.*) He's out there alright, mate. But round here he goes by the name of the Voots.

JIM: The Voots.

RON: The Voot family. An entire clan of the lowest, vilest, most violent and underhand hard nuts. Sly-groggers, loan sharks, thieves, cut-throats, murderers and extortionists – in short, enthusiastic race-goers to a man. And proud owners of said pony.

> *The penny starts to drop with* BAXTER. MORRIESON *nods.*

That's right. He may look like three hundred pounds of

best tripes now, but I can assure you this was a racehorse, mate!

JIM: You said the horse was on the road. Wandering. An accident . . .

RON: But are the Voots gonna see it that way? Benny Voot? Jack? Vance? Jesus, let's not even think about Vance . . .

Or are they gonna reckon it's a wee bit of a coincidence? Seeing as about ten hours from now – in the Voot scheme of things – this mount is supposed to be romping past the winning post of the prestigious and lucrative Hawera Handicap. And I don't think rigor mortis is the handicap they had in mind.

JIM: There's nothing to connect the horse to you.

RON: It's stuck in my bloody doorway!

JIM: That's where you wanted it!

RON: That is not where I wanted it! I wanted it winched into the frigging bastard porch! Safe from prying eyes! But I hadn't reckoned on you trying to break the land speed record in my backyard!

JIM: Why pick it up in the first place!

RON: I'll tell you. (MORRIESON *pushes* BAXTER *close to the horse carcass pointing out something.*) See that?

JIM: A tyre track.

RON: A very distinct not to mention distinctive tyre track. A 30-nought-50 in fact. Used exclusively in this burg on only two vehicles – my old flatbed Chrysler and the Volunteer Fire Brigade engine – which no doubt has an alibi.

JIM: Ah.

RON: Exactly! Our equine friend here is determined to stand as mute witness to his killers, pointing the hoof of blame unerringly in our direction and laughing. (*He kicks the horse. It farts.*)

JIM: Good luck, friend. For myself, I plan to be well out of town by daybreak.

As Baxter *climbs over the horse,* Morrieson *grabs his jacket and tries to pull him back.*

Ron: You can't just walk out! If this is pinned on me!

Jim: Drag your own horse! And leave me to drag mine!

Ron, *grappling with him*: I need your help!

Jim: I can't help you! I'm sick of being a bloody prophet. Sick of pounding my bones into bread for the crowd. I've given them my blood! But – like a child who knocks over his raspberry drink – they don't look at the mess they've made, they just want more!

Ron: You callous old bugger! (*Suddenly the phone begins to ring.* Morrieson *jumps.*) Who the hell? (*Motioning* Baxter *to be quiet and stay still,* Morrieson *picks up the phone.*) What's the idea of hauling a man out of his stretcher at this hour?

He listens a moment, turning his back, but then notices Baxter *quietly trying to slip out.*

Benny Voot.

Baxter *freezes in his tracks.*

Eh? Rustlers! Have to be some sort of big gambling outfit to pull a stunt like that, Benny. Probably miles away by now.

  Is that right? Oil on the road? Heading into town. So you've got the troops out. (*Unnoticed by* Baxter, Morrieson *cuts the connection with his finger, but keeps talking.*) Look, Benny I'd love to join the posse – you know me. Thing is I've been having a bit of a heavy session. Actual factual I'm that shickered I'm seeing horses right here in my own kitchen. Tell you what, mate – you know I'm on the corner of South Road and Regent – I'll keep a lookout, give you a tinkle if I see anything shady. Yeah, right as rain, Benny.

He hangs up. BAXTER *and* MORRIESON *gaze at each other a moment.* MORRIESON *gestures to the door.*

Go ahead, mate. (BAXTER *looks uncomfortable.*) You'd stick out like dog's balls round here at the best of times. Now, with the Voots out there combing the district, they'd have you down for a dead cert as a contract killer trying to leg it from the scene of the crime. A specialist horse hitman hired in from the city.

JIM, *speaking almost to himself, shaking his head*: Not yet. Not as I am. My sins unhealed – the dogs all round me with their mouths open. He has to give me time. Time to fix my mistakes, to mend my failures.

RON: I'll settle for time to get rid of the evidence. (*He takes a tablecloth out of a drawer.*) Give me a hand to draw a veil over proceedings in case anyone comes snooping round.

BAXTER *is beginning to get more of a grip on the situation.*

JIM: Hawera, you say?

RON: Hara.

JIM: And you?

RON: Me Ron.

BAXTER *solemnly shakes* MORRIESON'*s hand (again). He takes an end of the cloth and they drape it over the horse.* MORRIESON *takes an apron from another drawer and starts putting it on.*

We've gotta lose this horse where no bugger'll find him. One wave of our magic shovels and there'll be nothing left of Distant Waterway but a dent in the front fender and a late scratching.

JIM: Distant . . . ?

By this time MORRIESON *is also tying an apron round* BAXTER.

RON: Waterway. Named after old Ma Voot's favourite saying. Far canal. (*He goes to a large kitchen implement drawer and rummages inside.*) When it comes to digging a grave big enough without being noticed I reckon we've got two shows. No show and a shit show. Too risky to try and transport him. Even with a tarp over the top the Voots'll spot a load like that a mile away. Nope – we've gotta reduce this problem to manageable-sized pieces.

> MORRIESON *comes up with a series of implements. He gives* BAXTER *a cleaver and roasting fork.* MORRIESON *keeps a butcher's hacksaw and a large carving knife which he starts stropping against a steel.*

Not squeamish are you, mate? Beauty. I'll hold his legs – you carve.

> *They advance towards the horse.* MORRIESON *holds his hand up, and crushes out his smoke.*

Fags out. There's enough natural gas in there to blow us to kingdom come. (*As they move towards the horse again* MORRIESON *abruptly stops, gesturing for silence. They hear the door of the truck slam.*) Someone's out by the truck!

> MORRIESON *makes a flying leap at the light switch, plunging the scene into darkness.* MORRIESON *and* BAXTER *crouch down behind the draped horse, trying to stay absolutely quiet. Footsteps approach, hesitate, then pass the doorway and go off down the side of the house (possibly a figure is glimpsed passing the window).* MORRIESON *slowly puts his head up to peer out. Suddenly the door behind them opens and the* AUNT *enters.*

AUNT: Ronald!

RON, *startled*: Jesus!

He rises to meet her, uncomfortably aware that the owner of the footsteps is still in the vicinity.

I mean – watch out for the glass, Aunty.

AUNT: I've got my gardening boots on. What's happened to the light in here?

RON: Bulb's blown.

AUNT: There's spares in the cupboard.

RON, *preventing her heading in the direction of the wrecked cupboards*: Could be a fuse actually. I'll have a dekko in a minute. You just hop back in bed and—

AUNT: Why are you whispering, Ronald?

MORRIESON *is stuck for a moment, then coughs.*

RON: Bit of a cold coming on.

AUNT: I'm not surprised – out in the night air all hours. And I know you don't wear that scarf I knitted. You keep it in the truck and put it on before you come in the house. I don't know what your mother would say.

RON: What about you? Going walkabout in the middle of the night – you'll catch your death.

AUNT: You know where the Buckley's is.

RON: Same place it's been the last fifty years. Come on now, back in bed.

AUNT: Don't shoo me, Ronald. You'll make me forget what I came out for. Here. (*She flicks him the newspaper she is carrying.*) I want you to make sure you wrap the broken glass – thickly, Ronald.

RON, *shepherding her towards the door*: Will do, Aunty. Night-night.

AUNT *waits expectantly.* MORRIESON *kisses her.*

AUNT: Night-night.

She goes. MORRIESON *breathes a sigh of relief.*

RON: Jesus Christ, I thought for sure she'd— *[see the horse.]*

BAXTER *hisses at him for quiet.* MORRIESON *freezes. The footsteps outside are heard coming back. Once more they hesitate, then climb up the steps to the porch. A figure appears stealthily in the doorway.*

WILMA, *hoarsely*: Ron . . . ? Ron . . . ?

Finding the doorway blocked by the amorphous mound of the horse under the tablecloth, WILMA *tries to clamber over the obstacle but trips on the uneven footing and falls with an oath.*

Shit! (*Sprawled across the tablecloth-covered horse,* WILMA *flounders about until she rolls off –*) Jesus bloody Christ! (*– flattening* BAXTER, *whom she mistakes in the dark for* MORRIESON.) Ron! What the hell are ya playing at!

BAXTER *is pinned underneath her.*

When I saw the light go out I went down to your window. Ron? Are you alright? God, is he even breathing?

As she brings her face close to his, her scent sparks a recognition in BAXTER.

JIM: Pyrrha . . .
WILMA: Eh?

MORRIESON, *who has been standing back, switches the light on.* WILMA *takes one look at* BAXTER *and jumps a mile.*

Jesus! (*Leaping to her feet she stumbles away, pulling her skirt down.*)

RON, *to* BAXTER: A slight hitch. Remain calm whatever the provocation.

WILMA: Ron Morrieson, ya bastard!

> WILMA *is thirty-six, brassy without being a slut, in the local male parlance a 'player'. She smokes, drinks, gambles and sleeps with men she likes. She is honest (with herself and others) and, underneath the abrasiveness, vulnerable – especially to an awareness of the passing time and a narrowing of her options. If she feels attacked, however, she can retaliate with real venom.*

RON: Sshh!

WILMA: Who the bloody hell's this!

RON: You'll wake the old lady.

WILMA: Don't give me that old lady bull! I've had a gutsful of it! Climbing in and out of your friggin' bedroom window all hours!

RON: Wilma! I have company.

> *He indicates* BAXTER, *whom* WILMA *scorches with her glance.*

WILMA: Company! Another one of ya crumb-bums! Where'd ya dredge this one up?

> BAXTER *has been staring at* WILMA.

JIM: A strong ghost. In the dark, your scent . . .

WILMA: Thought I'd stumbled across ya corpse. Thought you'd crashed the truck and crawled in here to die.

RON: Sorry to disappoint you.

WILMA, *becoming almost plaintive*: Why didn't you come by like you said, Ron? I been stuck up home like a bastard on Father's Day.

RON, *waving his hand at her breath*: Giving the brandy bottle a spanking.

JIM, *realising*: Mingled perfume and cherry brandy.
    Her long legs under the blanket
    On a spring Saturday
    With a peach tree out in the yard . . .
WILMA: What's he going on about?
RON: How would I know? Poor bugger hasn't been able to get a
    word in edgeways since you came in.

> WILMA *rallies defiantly.*

WILMA: So come on then. What's goin' on? Eh?
RON: Pull ya head in, Wilma.
WILMA: Place looks like a bomb hit it.
RON: Nothin's going on.
WILMA, *turning back to the draped mound in the doorway*: And
    what's the big idea of this? I coulda broke my bloody neck!

> *She moves to lift the tablecloth.*

RON: Lift that cloth, Wilma – and I can't be held responsible for
    the consequences. (*The authority in his voice stops her.*)
WILMA: Don't tell me there's another stewbum under there?
    Sleeping it off. (*She shudders slightly.*) Jesus, I musta been
    lyin' right on top of him. Felt sorta – squashy – and damp
    . . . (*She feels the damp patch on her blouse. She realises with
    horror that it's blood. She backs away.*) It's not what I said?
    It's never a – a corpse?

> *As* BAXTER *opens his mouth,* MORRIESON *silences him.*

RON: Schtum.
WILMA: Cripes, Ron – what've ya done now! You haven't
    murdered someone? At least tell me it was an accident!
RON: It was an accident.
WILMA: Don't give me that! You've done for some poor bugger!
    The two of you! He looks like he'd slit ya throat as soon as
    look at ya!

Jim: No – don't be— *[frightened.]*

Wilma: You just bloody keep away from me! (*She backs off, looking to* Morrieson *for support.*) Ron?

Ron: You're a witness now, Wilma.

> Wilma's *eyes widen. She backs away and stumbles against the butcher's instruments, sending them clattering to the floor.* Wilma *goggles at them, terror-stricken beyond even bad language.*

Wilma: Aw, crumbs. (Wilma *snatches up the carving knife and holds it, trembling, in front of her.*) I'll scream. (*She backs towards the doorway and the dread mound.*) I'll scream bloody blue murder. I'll wake up the old lady.

Ron: What makes you think that isn't her under there?

Wilma: You wouldn't.

Ron: I reckon she's not quite conked yet, Wilma. Look out a bony hand doesn't reach out and clutch your ankle!

> Wilma's *foot touches the horse and she jumps away with a shriek.* Morrieson *bursts out laughing.*

Wilma, *realising*: You buggers. You been stringing me along. You bloody buggers! (*She whips the tablecloth off and recoils.*) What's that doing there!

Ron: Extra tea towel holder.

> *He mimes inserting a tea towel in the obvious socket.*

Wilma: Never mind playing silly buggers – what're you doing with a dead horse?

Ron ⎱ Flogging it.
Jim ⎰ Flogging it?

> Wilma *takes a different meaning from flogging.*

Wilma: I get it. You're gonna sell it to that screw-loose butcher mate of yours with his mystery pies. That's it, isn't it?

RON: No foxing a shrewdie like you, Wilma.

> WILMA *is suspicious at Morrieson's capitulation. But that's not the point.*

WILMA: I've got a bone to pick with you.
RON: Jeez, Wilma, I've got a guest.
WILMA: You said you were gonna come by. We got things to talk about.
RON: Tomorrow. We can talk tomorrow.
WILMA: You're full as a bull. Full of bull – as usual.
RON: Wilma . . .
WILMA: And you haven't even offered a girl a drink.

> *She heads for the booze but* MORRIESON *takes her arm.*

RON: Boys' night, eh? Boys' night.
WILMA, *flinging his arm off angrily*: Bugger you then!

> WILMA *turns to march out. The sound of* BAXTER'S *voice stops her.*

JIM: Let Time be still
    Who takes all things
    Face, feature, memory
    Under his blinding wings

    That I hold again the green
    Larch of your body . . .

> WILMA *stares at him.*

Please. Would you join us?
WILMA: At least someone's got a few manners. (*She comes back in, ignoring* MORRIESON. BAXTER *pours her a drink as* MORRIESON *watches them shrewdly.*) That was beauty.
RON, *rubbing his hands together*: Just about time for a feed I

reckon. Dunno about you but I could . . . (*He glances at the horse.*) No offence, mate!

He goes to the electric frypan on the bench and starts frying a large amount of bacon.

JIM: There was a woman I wrote that for. You put me in mind of her.

WILMA: She live round here? I got heaps of cousins.

JIM: Your mouth was the sun
And green earth under
The rose of your body flowering
Asking and tender
In the timelost season
Of perpetual summer.

WILMA: Why don't you never say things like that, Ron?

JIM: To me she was Pyrrha. All women in one woman. I didn't know then how short life is. How few the ones who really touch us.

WILMA, *to* BAXTER: He calls hisself a writer.

RON, *fabricating quickly*: Coupla articles for the paper. Local history.

WILMA: Most of what he says ya couldn't print. I told him if that's your idea of literature half the cockies round here are bloody Shakespeare!

RON: Too right, Wilma. And you're an opera singer.

WILMA: I'm a *torch* singer!

RON: Got news for you then, girl. Your bulb's blown and your batteries are flat.

WILMA, *sticking out her chest*: Not what you were saying last night. (*To* BAXTER.) I useta sing with Ron's combo – dances and twenty-firsts right across the district. Ron'd introduce me as the Taranaki Tui.

RON: Talk about a voice to shatter glass. She'd start up and the bottles'd be flying in no time.

WILMA: I gave the band a bit of class.

RON: Or something rhyming with that.

> WILMA *drains her glass and* BAXTER *refills it.*

WILMA: What happened with your lady friend. You know, whose mouth was the sun and all that?

JIM: Left me for a ginger-haired clod who could do it four times a night. (WILMA *clucks sympathetically.*)
Remember, Pyrrha – it's much the same whether
You kiss his mouth or his arse – the same
Dull buttock-face, the same shitty breath,
The same red tuft of hair.

> WILMA *laughs.*

WILMA: That's a good one! Put a girl right off!

JIM: Pity I didn't think of it at the time.

WILMA: Could've used that myself at some of those twenty-firsts we played, eh Ron?

Remember that old bus you had? You'd pull up outside the Egmont Hotel on a Saturday night. The band'd all pile in and off we'd go. All in our best. Passing round a flask in the back to get us warmed up. Me with butterflies like I was going to a ball or something instead of some haybarn out Kaponga way. Saturday night meant something then. People knew how to enjoy themselves.

Seems like an age since I heard you play the piano, Ron.

> WILMA *goes over to the piano, opens the lid and inexpertly hits a couple of keys.*

RON: Leave it.

WILMA: Come on, Ron. Give us one of the old tunes.

> *She starts to sing 'Ain't Misbehavin'' while plunking the*

odd key. MORRIESON *simmers for a line or two, then reacts angrily.*

RON: I said leave it!

WILMA *does.* MORRIESON *returns to his cooking.*

WILMA: We've gotta talk, Ron.

RON, *evasively*: I've been grogging on a bit, Wilma.

WILMA: I want to know if you meant what you said last night.

RON: We can talk tomorrow, eh? (MORRIESON *turns away, opening a couple of cupboards.*)

WILMA: What if I said tonight or nothing?

RON, *pretending he hasn't heard this*: No cackleberries. Man can't have a fry-up under these conditions.

WILMA: Ron?

RON: I'll just – see what I can do to rectify the situation. (*He heads for the door.*)

WILMA: Old Cyril Thompson reckons if he catches the bugger that's been lifting his eggs he'll be picking pellets out of his bum till New Year's.

RON: That right? Better do the neighbourly thing and swing by Old Cyril's place while I'm out – make sure everything's secure. (*He looks at* BAXTER *and taps his nose.*) See how the land lies.

MORRIESON *goes.*

WILMA: Ron! (WILMA *looks after him suspiciously. She crosses to the cupboards and comes up with some eggs.*) Eggs my bum! (WILMA *looks at the bacon Morrieson has left frying, gives it a stir.*)

If he thinks he can get out of it that easy he's got another think coming. Bugger needs a rocket under him. (*As she cracks the eggs into the frypan she takes a second look at* BAXTER.) Now I know where I've seen you. You're that poet fella, aren't ya? From that – what do you call it – up the Wanganui River.

JIM: Hiruharama.

WILMA: Nah – commune.

JIM: Jerusalem.

WILMA: That's it. Seen you in *Truth*.

JIM: *Truth, Truth, Truth, Truth,*
You'll do to wipe my arse
You'll do to light the fire at night
But I read you for a laugh

WILMA: I hear it's pretty up the river in springtime. What's it like this time of year?

JIM: Bloody cold and not enough to eat.

WILMA: Reckon that'd put a stop to all that prancing round in the nuddy. Best kept for the summer, eh? All that love and beads stuff.

BAXTER *moves round behind her as she cooks.*

JIM: The thought of your body
Sets me in mind of the white
Cataract or goddess –

WILMA: That right?

JIM: Leaping two thousand feet from Lake Quill
Down to the green womb
Of the bush below – (*He touches her.*)

WILMA: That bush is closed to trampers. (*She shrugs him off.*) Anyway – I thought those hippie sheilas were more your style? Getting a bit long in the tooth to start painting flowers on my tits.

BAXTER *cups her breasts from behind.*

JIM: My journey's end
Two breasts like towers –

WILMA, *removing his hands*: Maybe, when it comes down to it,

you prefer a bit of nylon stocking. A woman who knows
the score.

JIM: If eighteen men climbed up your bush track before me,
Well, I'm the lucky nineteenth!

WILMA: That what Ron's been saying about me?

JIM, *grabbing her*: I'm in the saddle now
Riding the tornado!

> BAXTER *pulls her round to face him, trying to kiss her, but
> as* WILMA *turns she delivers a crushing knee to his balls. He
> staggers away, doubled over.*

WILMA: Well I reckon now you know better!

> BAXTER *has sunk, bent up, into a chair. Pause.* WILMA
> *pushes the eggs around the pan.*

I just don't like people jumping to conclusions.

JIM: Can't see myself jumping anywhere in the near future.

WILMA: Sorry.

JIM: At least it proves they haven't entirely shriveled away. If
it came to the crunch you'd have been safe, d'ye see? I've
found a prophet's life to be hard in every way but one.

WILMA: Jesus, men. Whether it's up or whether it's down you
think the world revolves around it, don't ya?

JIM: Not always.

WILMA: Always.

JIM: I could tell you a story. When I was in Thailand once—

WILMA: Don't worry – I been told stories by the best of them.
Ron's a bloody world champion. Every one a pearler. (*She
goes off on her own concerns.*) Well, he's not wriggling out
this time. And he can have a dose of his own medicine.
Keep an eye out will ya? Sing out when you see him coming
back.

> *Glancing at* BAXTER, WILMA *realises she has cut him off
> and relents.*

Go on, then. Tell me your story.

JIM: And be one more storyteller?

WILMA: Make it the truth and I'll enjoy the novelty.

BAXTER *hesitates.*

Where was it you said?

JIM: Thailand. Bangkok. Now there's a city whose name speaks its nature. (*He ponders.*) While I was there I felt the world did revolve around Bangkok. A vortex, drawing everything down to the root.

My last night – as black and hot as the inside of a boiler. Suffocating, I stepped onto the street for air, and a girl with a ribbon in her hair took my arm. I remember her ribbon. All the sadness and the hope of the world fluttering in it. To tie something pretty in your hair the better to sell your body . . . I looked at her – told her 'no thanks, honey'.

WILMA, *not unaffected*: Want a medal, do you?

JIM: Felt I deserved one. I invited her to eat with me. She was poor and desperate. As well as she could, she told me her troubles. I took out all the money I had and put it on the table. Divided it in half, and we each took our share. Now, I thought, I can sleep. Now she can go home . . . (*He trails off.*)

WILMA: You married? (BAXTER *nods.*) Family?

JIM: A girl and a boy – both grown. A granddaughter now.

WILMA: Lovely.

JIM: Times with them, I've felt the possibility of peace tug at the very roots of my soul. There was wood to be chopped – fences to be mended. My granddaughter to be tucked down at night, shouting and playing a game of kicking off the covers.

WILMA: Nothing like family.

JIM, *face darkening*: And I knew – equally knew in my water that

all this – this 'peace' – would strangle my life like a vine
chokes a tree. I remember watching a television programme
on yachting, thinking: as I sit here the heads of the poor
are being smashed on the walls of prison cells. Seeing
out my window the blue flickering light in every window
– the whole echo cage and mirror house of the mass media
freezing the heart.

WILMA: So it's a choice between freezing your heart at home and
freezing your arse up the Wanganui?

JIM: I come from Dunedin. My arse has permafrost.

WILMA: You don't get on with your wife.

BAXTER *shrugs*.

JIM: She wants a husband. Understandable – given we're married.
Why should she accept that I was called? If she didn't hear
it herself. All she sees is a man getting out of her warm bed,
letting the chill in. Needlessly. But that's it, d'ye see? The
need. *Their* need. Nga mokai, nga raukore – the orphans of
this world. The ones who've had their leaves and branches
stripped by the heavy winds of junk, alcohol, prison . . .

WILMA: Then why aren't ya there now? Jerusalem?

JIM, *sagging*: There was – a conference. Down south.

WILMA: Bit out of your way up here.

JIM: I spoke about the poor. About suffering. I spoke at length
on love. All the while I could see my words turning into
grey ash as they left my mouth. And in the still moment
of silence, before the applause and the slaps on the back
and cups of tea with earnest undergraduates and groovy
clergymen, a voice said – it could have been out of the back
row, but I knew it leaked from the very back teeth of my
soul – 'You liar.'

And then that voice became my mantra. All the long
journey back I heard it, as if it was naming the nine million
names of God. But they were all me. All the same name.

Liar.

    I was dropped at the turn-off. A mile away at Jerusalem waited my family – my second family, my orphans. At the end of the shingle road the colour of ash they were waiting for their prophet to save them. To give them a word, a sign, something they could believe in. To give them above all, beneath all, love.

    I began walking the other way.

WILMA: How d'ya like your eggs?

JIM: That was I think the day before yesterday. I haven't slept. I haven't stopped. For fear of death.

WILMA: Sunnyside up. No point coming here to hide from death. Hawera's the first place he'll look.

JIM: I know now. Mine has been the worst failure – the failure to love.

WILMA: You might be a ringer for John the Baptist but if you ask me it's your wife who's got the patience of a saint. If you knew what was good for ya you'd forget the hippie jailbait, dump the doom and gloom and get back home to your wife and kids! Some of us ain't even got what you turn your nose up at! Someone to love ya and take care of ya. Here. (*She scrapes the bacon and eggs onto a plate and slaps it in front of* BAXTER.)

    Come on, get that down ya. Ya can't just sit around guzzling booze all night.

JIM: I'm a reformed alcoholic, woman. A member of AA for fourteen years.

WILMA, *genuinely surprised*: Are ya? Ya look as pissed as a newt.

There is the sound of a shotgun blast in the distance.

Jesus! That's Ron. Cyril Thompson's done for him. Oh my God! (*She peers out the window.*) No. Here he comes now.

Her alarm turns to determination.

Right. I'll give the bugger something to think about!

To BAXTER's *surprise and confusion* WILMA *grabs him and kisses him passionately. She hitches up her skirt and straddles him. She slaps his hands on her thighs and buries his face between her breasts.*

Yes, yes, oh yes! You know how to do things to a girl! You're just all man!

MORRIESON *stands in the doorway surveying this scene, dumbfounded. He stands on the horse to get a better view.* WILMA *pretends to be too caught up in her amorous entanglement to notice his presence.*

RON: You bloody horny shaggy old bugger. (WILMA *breaks off kissing* BAXTER *and looks at* MORRIESON *defiantly.*) I've seen some prize pricks in my time, mate, but you'd have to be right up with the field! To prong a man's girlfriend in his own kitchen while he's out rustling up some grub for ya! You've got more cheek than an elephant's bum!

WILMA: Cheers, Ron. That's the first time you've called me your girlfriend.

RON: And as for you, Wilma—

WILMA: Don't you look at me in that tone of voice, Ron Morrieson!

RON: Well I'm stonkered. You, you disappoint me, Wilma. It's enough to make a man sick as a pig with life in general.

WILMA *climbs off* BAXTER.

WILMA: You can cut the bull, Ron! This'd suit you just fine, wouldn't it? It'd get you off the hook nicely!

RON: What're you talking about?

WILMA: If you think I'm going to hang round like a half-sucked blackball waiting for you to get the guts up to give me the shove!

Ron: Sshh!

Wilma: Bugger the old lady! It's my thirty-seventh birthday a
bloody fortnight on Tuesday! So you just stand up like a
man and give me the story or I'm out that door for good,
Ron! (*She is in tears.*) And you can play that over on ya
ukulele!

> Baxter *has had a growing awareness of something. Now*
> *he looks down his trousers.*

Jim: I've got a hard on.

Ron: Listen, mate – (Morrieson *catches* Baxter's *attention and*
nods towards the door.) – how about standing sentry for a
bit?

> Baxter *gets the message and lurches out the back door,*
> *clambering over the horse. Silence.* Morrieson *seems*
> *sobered.* Wilma *blows her nose.*

Wilma: I meant what I said last night.

Ron: I know you did.

Wilma: I thought you did too. Then you don't come round – I
ring up and you give me some gobbledygook! What the hell
was all that on the phone?

Ron: I've had a couple of things on my mind.

Wilma: Too right, boozing and more boozing! You can't look
after yourself. You'll be back in the hospital in no time.

I don't wanna live out my life alone, Ron. I want a
husband. I want some kids.

I'm offering to take you on. I got no friggin' pride
left! Just say something, will ya! If it's because you think
everyone'd laugh at ya, if ya wanna join half the jokers in
town in crossing the street when they see me comin', then
for God's sake— [*say so.*]

Ron: A man'd be lucky to have you as his wife, Wilma. Any

bastard should be as proud as a dog with two pricks. You're a great girl.

WILMA: I'm no girl. And let's face it, neither one of us is any oil painting. But we know each other, don't we? We can put up with each other, can't we?

Christ, it's not as if I'm asking you to give up the turps or anything. I'll take ya as you are – with ya big talk, grand schemes – and ya bloody stupid great big heart!

RON: It's not to do with you. Nothing on your side of the fence, Wilma.

WILMA: Then what is it? What!

A look of infinite sadness passes over MORRIESON's *face. He turns away, towards the piano and the photo of his mother.* WILMA *touches him gently.*

She's dead, Ron. Dead.

MORRIESON *closes the lid of the piano, biting back tears.*

It's one thing to let it stop you playing the piano, but you gotta get on with your life. (*He puts an arm out to* WILMA *blindly. She hugs him into her tightly, fiercely.*) This town! This bloody fuckin' town! It's like a stone on top of us! We could shift away. Go someplace else.

RON, *pulling away, composing himself*: What are ya talking about, woman? I love Hawera. I was born here, I'm gonna— *[die here.]*

Nowhere else like it.

WILMA: Marry me, Ron. It's leap year, isn't it? So I can ask.

MORRIESON *looks at her.*

RON: Bugger it. Why not?

WILMA: That's what you said last night. If it's just the grog talking I won't be crawling back tomorrow for more. Even I've got a limit, Ron.

RON: Just promise me one thing. After we're married you'll still climb in our bedroom window every night. I don't reckon I could get a silly on without seeing you panting and struggling, your bazooms all squashed against the window sill. It's better than a nudie show.

WILMA: You mad bugger! (*She embraces and kisses him.*) You'll see, Ron, it'll be corker, the two of us. I'll look after ya, feed you up, make sure you take your pills.

RON: Speaking of feeds, this calls for a celebratory re-fry-up.

MORRIESON *takes the untouched plate of bacon and eggs, scrapes it back into the frypan and starts cooking it again.*

WILMA: What're you doing with that Baxter joker?

RON, *giving her a sly look*: Baxter? Said he had some Maori name.

WILMA: You know exactly who he is.

RON, *grinning*: Just having a yarn. Lucky bugger's got the lot. Doesn't even know he's born.

WILMA: You'll have the same – wife, family . . .

That's not what MORRIESON *means.*

RON: Books! You couldn't jump over what he's had published. Got all the standing with the literary critters you could wish for . . .

WILMA: You can start your writing again. Even if we have kids, I'll keep them quiet when you're on your typewriter.

RON: Nah, I'm finished with that. I'll take up a more honest hobby – french knitting, or Satanism.

WILMA: Don't hand me that, Ron Morrieson. If you get a hot thing going behind my back, I know it'll be with this old Olympia. (*She uncovers the typewriter.*) You got something in here already, ya lying hound.

MORRIESON *looks up, concerned, as* WILMA *picks up the*

short story from on top of the typewriter.

'The Guitar Lesson'.
RON: It's just a short story.

But WILMA *has flicked a page or two and recognised it.*

WILMA: Hey, this is you!
RON, *coming towards her to take it*: Give it here will ya, Wilma?
WILMA: This is about that time I caught you fooling round with that tart of a schoolgirl.
RON: I don't want anyone reading it yet.
WILMA: What d'ya want to write about that for? People'll think you're a pervo. (*She flicks more pages.*) Am I in here?
RON: Not exactly.

He tries to take the story but WILMA *evades him.*

WILMA: Here we go. 'Dulcie,' – Dulcie! – 'my girlfriend who'd been chasing me for eighteen months'?

She darts an uncertain look at MORRIESON.

RON: Look, Wilma—

WILMA's *reading of the next sentence has the hollow resounding tone of a nail going into a coffin.*

WILMA: 'I had no intention of marrying Dulcie because her family was downright common and she could swear like a bullock driver.'

WILMA *puts the manuscript down.*

So.
RON: Wilma!
WILMA: Well, at least you talk straight to that typewriter. Christ knows, when it comes to me you can't find two words of the truth to rub together.

RON: Come on, Wilma. It's only a story.

WILMA: I knew I wasn't considered to be quite the bill of goods. I've got used to your aunt sailing past me in the street like I was something she might get on her shoe. I just never thought – it never crossed my mind – that was how you felt too.

RON: I don't!

> WILMA *gestures at the piano and photo of Morrieson's mother.*

WILMA: It's her isn't it? Your mum told you not to marry me, didn't she? Eh? (MORRIESON *looks torn and tormented.*) She's dead – but she still wouldn't like it. That's the guts of it, isn't it, Ron?

RON: Jeez, Wilma!

WILMA: But I'm good enough for a quick tumble when you're grogged up and the tanks are full. (*She brandishes the story.*) Or for having a good laugh at! (*She throws it down, the pages scattering, her hurt hardening into anger.*) Well you can rot! Hear me! The idea of you looking down your nose at anyone! It makes me wanna laugh my ring out! Look at ya – in ya dirty old overcoat – you're nothing but a dero!

RON: This coat suited you fine when you had your bare bum on it beside the truck last night.

WILMA: Years I bloody wasted! On you! You with ya 'I'm a writer, doncha know'. No wonder the library won't stock your book.

RON: Books!

> WILMA *grabs Morrieson's copy of* The Scarecrow *from the bookshelf.*

WILMA: Woman there reckons you could read a better class of smut in the railway station bogs! And I bloody stood up for

ya! Well she's right – who wants to read the ravings of some
sick, dero alkie who just fluked it once!

RON: Twice! And it was no fluke!

> WILMA *drops the book.*

WILMA: Ya haven't given a music lesson in a year! If you're not
draped over her grave – ya tryna drink yourself into yours!
Or bullshitting everyone down the pub! Mr Ron Morrieson
– local personality – what a dag! That's all you're cut out to
be – a big turd in a small sewage pond!

RON: And who's this floating by? Some old used frenchie split at
the seams. Hi, Wilma!

> WILMA *goes white and cold with fury. She puts her coat on
> and heads for the door.*

Wilma!

> WILMA *swings back to nail him with a curse.*

WILMA: You – done nothing! Are nothing! Crack on you love it
here but the truth is you've always been too gutless to poke
your nose outside. Well now you can die here. In your own
shit. And I'll be round to laugh when you do.

> WILMA *stalks out.* MORRIESON *has been powerfully affected
> by her curse. He looks pale and shaken. He staggers to the
> door and calls after her.*

RON: Wilma. (*She obviously keeps on walking.* MORRIESON *is
struck with a jolting spasm of pain in his guts.*) Jesus!

> *He reels away, finds his bottle of pills on the sink bench
> and swallows a few. He collapses at the table, his head on
> his arms, his breath coming in tearing ragged gasps – but
> whether sobbing from grief, from pain, or just trying
> to steady his breathing and ride out the attack is not*

apparent. After a moment BAXTER *appears in the doorway and clambers inside again.*

JIM: No sign of any Voots. (*He slumps into a chair.*) I'm sorry your woman friend has gone. There was something I wanted to tell her.

> *Wrapped up in his own story,* BAXTER *pays scant attention to* MORRIESON.

She was right of course. In Thailand that night, the woman I shared my money with walked me back to my hotel. I felt scoured, at peace with the world. But when we reached the hotel, as I turned to wish her good luck, she touched me. Here. (*He puts his hand lightly on his crotch.*)

We went to her shack. I remember the lights through the bamboo blind.

Much as I try, I can't regret the story had a different ending to the one I might have wished. The next day in the crowded airport a great blue and red lizard fell from the ceiling onto my shoulder. I felt my sex had been returned to me. That I'd been reborn, remade in the steaming oven of that night – Chinese cards scattered on a hard mattress – naked inside a naked girl with a ribbon in her hair.

Your lady seems to share some of the same magic. A type of magnetism in her box with curious effects upon old and rusted lumps of iron ore – the moon pulling seaweed tides over ancient shipwrecks. Unfortunately her good sense put me in mind of my mother – a woman to whom I am careful never to tell the whole story.

Still – after all my failures, all the calamities, even running blindly under the black edge of death – I can't shed my simple human wish to be loved.

Tell me, little one,
That my body is strong, that my hands are clean,

That my heart has in it a seed of light,
Then let me come beside you and hide myself
In the darkness of the garden of the sorrow of your face.

> *After a moment,* BAXTER *idly picks up the copy of* The
> Scarecrow *dropped by Wilma.* MORRIESON *raises his head
> in time to see* BAXTER *read the first sentence – and snort
> – sealing his fate.* BAXTER *glances up to find* MORRIESON
> *staring at him balefully.*

RON: You want death? I'll give you death.

> MORRIESON *rises suddenly, and takes the book from*
> BAXTER. *Crossing to the stove, he scrapes the contents of
> the frypan back onto the plate, then puts the plate in front
> of* BAXTER. *As* BAXTER *moves to partake –*

Jack Voot's been shot. (BAXTER *stops, staring at* MORRIESON.)
You must've heard it. I've had a hell of a shock, I can tell
you. You mind?

> MORRIESON *pulls the untouched plate towards him and
> samples an egg. He reaches into a pocket without result.
> Looks round.*

Seen my smokes?

> *Throughout what follows* MORRIESON *manages to consume
> the entire contents of the plate in addition to drinking,
> talking and smoking a butt out of the ashtray.*

I'm just taking a wander round Old Cyril Thompson's
place, after a fresh egg or two – in the interests of being
a decent host I might add. I get round the corner of the
fowlhouse and come groin to muzzle with a bloody shotgun!
There's Old Man Thompson himself parked up in his
creaky old wheelchair. My heart was kicking the sides out
of my neck. I just about did my laundry on the spot. But

blow me tight if the bugger wasn't asleep.

Crazy old coot's been obsessed with trespassers ever since us kids'd sneak down to his creek trying to snare his eels. The local legend was they'd grown huge on the offal Old Cyril chucked in.

Well, the shadow had nothing on me as I slipped out of that locale. But I'd no sooner hit the street when I was pinned dead on by headlights.

I recognised the car straightaway by its shape like a shark – and the sinister way it cruised. It was the Voot Coupe – owner one Jack Voot esquire – and it was on the hunt for horsenappers.

I folded my tent like a shaky arab – but as I ducked back up Old Man Thompson's path I heard the anchors go on the Coupe, Jack Voot yelling out to stop, then the racket of him coming up behind me.

I was almost to the fowlhouse when I remembered what was laying round the corner – on this particular starry night a lot more than the prize Black Orpingtons – namely Mad Cyril making love to a fully cocked 12-gauge. I took a flier sideways off the path and rolled through a hole in the hedge. Jack Voot went past like an express train and round the side of the hen-house. The rate he was going he would have run straight into Old Cyril. You must have heard the blast from here.

JIM: Dead?

RON: By what I saw it'll be a closed casket. Brush and shovel job.

JIM: The old man?

> BAXTER *makes a move to stand.* MORRIESON *grabs him by the elbow, shaking his head.*

RON: The wheelchair was lying on its back, wheels still spinning. The collision added to the recoil must've somersaulted him backwards down the gully and into the creek. I took a look down. Mate, I almost puked. That water was alive. I reckon Old Cyril's fed those eels for the last time. (BAXTER *stares at this vision of horror.*) Hemi, I reckon we're in deep shit. And it's setting like concrete.

JIM: Each man eaten by the thing he feeds. The eels in the black creek of his soul. There's a poem in that.

RON: You gotta help me, mate! Come morning the rozzers are going to be all over this town like ants!

JIM: The fuzz.

RON: I could give the Ds the whole song and dance – but who'd believe me? They've had so many backhanders from the Voots they've developed tennis elbow! But what else can I do? Sit here while their relentless investigations inch them closer and closer?

JIM: But every light on the ceiling of the room
Is the light of a squad car
Every noise –
Means for him the fuzz are at the door –

BAXTER *rises, getting more and more into it.*

To break the locks, brother,
To tear down the wallpaper,
To empty the cupboards onto the carpet!

RON: Steady on, mate.

JIM: Suddenly you see them in the centre of the room –
The servants of the Zombie King!
Skorbul the football player with his brown moustache,
Krubble, who has a habit of crushing fingers in doors!

RON: There's only one cop in Hawera.

JIM: Drooble, who is glad to bang girls' heads on walls!

RON: Actually his name is Huggins and he lives right next door!
So if you wouldn't mind not waking the bugger up!

JIM: I have a problem with authority.

RON: You will, mate – cos if the shit hits the fan you can bet it'll splatter. That's three mysterious deaths you're involved in, counting Distant Waterway. (*He paces.*) There's no way I can keep the lid on this – Voots or cops – either way I'm marked for the meatworks.

There's only one thing to do.

BAXTER *nods.*

JIM: We will go to these Voots.
RON: Are you barking mad?
JIM: We will explain everything.

MORRIESON *pushes him back into his seat.*

RON: Look . . . look . . . Even if you did manage to catch Benny Voot totally by surprise with this novel approach – this fronting up and telling the truth thing – even if you could square it with his mother – who makes *Psycho* look like *The Sound of Music* – you'd still have one big problem. A problem even the two of them put together can't control. Vance Voot.
JIM: Vance Voot?
RON: I remember the day Vance had his accident. I was a year or two behind him at school. He was just your common or garden junior psychopath then. Vance pinched a detonator from the Ngahinetapu Quarry. Tripped over with it on the railway line and did as good a job as you could imagine of blowing his face off. Took out half his throat too so he's never spoke since.

After he got out of the hospital he just stayed up the farm. The one time he came into town, for a court case, kids who saw him in the street had nightmares for weeks. I hear even his brothers scoot round him like he's a hand grenade with a loose pin. Cut off from human contact there's only one thing in all the world that he loves – and which returned that love. (*He pauses for effect before directing* BAXTER's *eyes to the horse.*)

Raised it from a foal. (*He shudders and gets up, starting to pace, almost panicky.*) The idea of Vance Voot on my hammer. I tell you, it doesn't bear thinking about. (*He beats his pockets.*) Seen my cigarette case? Had it with me when I went out.

No, mate, there's only one way out of this and it's signposted State Highway 3.

I'll grab a few things and we'll hit the road. Have to take our chances dodging the Voot dragnet. Just hope the truck—

> MORRIESON *suddenly freezes, looking out through the open back door.*

JIM: What is it?

RON: Nothing. Jumping at shadows. Thought I . . . Jesus! (*He recoils, pushing* BAXTER *back.*) There's someone out there. Up against the fenceline.

> *He switches the light off. Moonlight comes in the window faintly illuminating the scene. They are breathing heavily in the darkness.*

It's probably just Wilma out there packing a sad. I'll sort it out. You keep your head down.

> MORRIESON *scrambles out the back door. His voice is heard from outside.*

RON, *off*: Oi! Who's that? Step out in the moonlight, mate. Let me see your face. (*There is a sound of movement, footsteps on the gravel.* MORRIESON's *voice, when it continues, is a little shaky.*) Vance. You nearly scared the tripe out of me.

> BAXTER *retreats, crouching, into a corner.*

Heard you'd had a bit of trouble. Only sorry I'm so off my face – no offence, Vance – that I can only get myself vertical to stagger out here to the dunny . . . Which, which as you can see we pulled down a few years ago when we got the new one inside. But – old habits, eh? Still like to piddle on the old spot. You wouldn't have a smoke on you would you, Vance?

Well, bugger me days, where'd you find my cigarette case? Musta dropped it somewhere on my travels. Looks like the smokes are on me then, eh? Got a light?

There is suddenly the deafening explosion of a shotgun blast just outside the door. Something clangs on the kitchen floor in the moonlight. It is MORRIESON's *cigarette case. Silence. Heavy footsteps crunch on gravel, then begin to mount the steps to the porch.* BAXTER, *huddled in his corner, begins quietly but hurriedly to recite his rosary. The menacing silhouette of* VANCE VOOT *appears, swathed in a long coat, hat pulled down over his eyes, face muffled. Finding the horse, he hesitates a moment and touches it. There is a wet gulping noise as* VANCE *takes a moment to grieve. Then he comes on into the kitchen. He stands in the shadow just inside the door – his breathing can be heard as a regular wet gurgling sound. He has a shotgun dangling from one hand. He swings his heavy head back and forth snuffing the air, zeroing in on* BAXTER. *As* VANCE VOOT *steps towards his hiding place* BAXTER *rises to meet him.*

JIM: You . . . Te Taipo . . . bush demon . . . as old and shrunken as I am, stubbornly braced in the mouth of my grave like a climber in a rock chimney, still I defy you. Death, I will wrestle with you!

BAXTER *jumps at* VOOT *and they struggle for possession of the shotgun. A struggle which* VOOT *inexorably wins,*

arching BAXTER *backwards over the piano, remorselessly
pressing the barrel of the shotgun down across his throat.*
VOOT *brings his terrible faceless face close to* BAXTER *– and
lets out a belch. He whips off his disguise. It is of course*
MORRIESON.

RON: Gidday mate! (*He laughs uproariously at his stunt and flicks
the light on.*) Had you going, didn't I? Eh? Eh!

JIM: Going?

RON: Got you tangled up good and proper! Voots! Horses!

JIM: It's only a story?

RON: Only! You were shitting yourself, you gloomy old
bastard!

JIM: But the horse?

RON: That's the best touch! Saw it lying on the side of the road!
Musta fell off a truck on the way to the knacker's yard! No
more a racehorse than I am!

JIM: You bloody maniac!

RON: Recognised you straight off. Was cudgeling the old
brainbox for a yarn to spin ya – when I spotted him! The
perfect literary device to squeeze your nuts in, eh? See who's
the top writer!

JIM: Writer?

RON: Who d'ya think you're dealing with? Ronald Hugh bloody
Morrieson, mate! That's who! Author of *The Scarecrow*! (*He
brandishes the book under* BAXTER'S *nose.*) And *Came a Hot
Friday*! (*He brandishes the second book in the same way.*)
    And I just outwrote you, mate! I showed you what a
story's all about!

        BAXTER *is outraged.*

JIM: You kidnap me, keep me here, just to prove you're a better
writer?

RON, *nodding delightedly, the picture of triumph*: You gotta laugh!
Don't ya? Eh? (*He pokes* BAXTER – *who gives a fake kind of*

half laugh.) Cos now we got that out of the way –

He suddenly fells BAXTER *with a short vicious blow to the belly from the shotgun. He steps on* BAXTER'S *arm and thrusts the muzzle of the shotgun into his face.*

– it really is time for you to die.

Blackout.

Act Two

Some time later. BAXTER *is standing on a footstool with a noose around his head. He is close to the inside door so as to be positioned under a hook on the ceiling. The rope runs tautly through this hook, along to another hook above the back door and down to the carcass of the horse which has now been raised a foot or two with a rickety arrangement involving a car or truck jack. When this is released the weight of the horse will hoist* BAXTER *into the air.* MORRIESON's *packed suitcase sits in the middle of the room.* MORRIESON *is adjusting the apparatus.*

RON: I mean – put yourself in my position.

> *He lets the jack down slightly, pulling* BAXTER *up onto the balls of his feet.* MORRIESON *takes a gulp from the bottle of whisky. He is flushed, his eyes bright. He is now well pissed.*

I write a bloody book, and a bloody good yarn it is too. No, no, no. Fuck ya, it is. (*He picks up* The Scarecrow.) *The Scarecrow* – by R. H. Morrieson. I saw ya.
   I saw ya! You opened this book – read the first sentence – and laughed!

JIM: Well . . .

RON: Same as every other smart bastard on the so-called literary scene. Same as the dickhead who reviewed it for the *Listener*. Hick from the sticks makes a hash of writing a book! Eh? Right from the first sentence. 'The same week our fowls were stolen, Daphne Moran had her throat cut.' Well, you may bloody laugh – but I happen to think that's funny!

JIM: So do— *[I.]*

> *This is cut off as* MORRIESON *lowers the jack again, pulling* BAXTER *up further.*

RON: The Aussies reckoned I wrote like an outback Charles Dickens. But what did I get here? In the land of my own birth? Five-eighths of fuck all! *Land*-bloody-*fall* wouldn't even review it. (*He puts* The Scarecrow *under* BAXTER's *feet, giving him slight respite.*)
So I wrote another one. (*He picks up* Came a Hot Friday.)
Wes Pennington. His faithful Cyril. Don and his poor old dad. The characters of a Russian novel! But one where you crack a smile. Can't stand a book where you don't crack a smile. The Te Whakinga Kid! I pissed myself writing him! When he . . . I won't spoil the plot, mate.
And what'd the smarty, arty farty literati make of that one, eh? 'This is not the New Zealand I know,' says some prick on the radio with a carrot up his arse!

He drops the jack again. BAXTER *tries to adjust to his precarious situation.*

At least that one made it into print. (*He places* Came a Hot Friday *under* BAXTER's *feet, then takes out a typed manuscript.* MORRIESON *is getting a little maudlin.*)
'Predicament'. Cedric, fat Mervyn Toebeck, The Spook. The Mystery of the Watcher in the Tower. A lonely boy coming of age. (*He shakes his head.*) Buggers won't publish it. Not here, not in Aussie. (*He pauses dangerously, his hand on the jack.*)
Now you on the other hand – a poet, a man of 'serious concerns' – anything you wanna scribble on the side of a fag packet is in print faster than a rat up a drainpipe. You've only got to fart and there's a publisher to say, 'How do you spell that?'

JIM: It's a view I'm not unfamiliar with.

RON: You've got no right to be miserable! The moment I saw you – staggering along the side of the road, playing at being

Moses in the wasteland. Bullshit! (*He adds the manuscript to the pile of paper under* BAXTER's *feet*.) There's the wasteland, mate! My life! My life's work!

Now you can find out what it's like. To be left hanging in midair! Cos you couldn't ever pile up enough to get a decent footing. Cos every time you thought you were getting somewhere they raised the ante!

He drops the jack again, stretching BAXTER *to the utmost.*

Here you go – (*He finds a final couple of manuscripts*.) – one last halfway-finished novel with no hope. And a couple of short stories. (*He adds Wilma's short story and sticks them under* BAXTER's *precariously perched feet*.)

Hang on – (*He removes the top short story again and picks up a pencil*.) – had a good line before. (*He remembers his retort to Wilma and writes in the margin a couple of pages in*.)

'Didn't mind this coat when you had your bare bum on it.'

He circles the sentence and draws an arrow to show where it should go in the text. Satisfied, he slips the short story back under BAXTER's *feet and stands back to look at the improvised gallows.*

My collected works. Meant everything to me. And now they mean everything to you.

JIM: I find them to be quite sound – though perhaps a little short.

RON, *eagerly*: You mean you've read them? You've heard of me?

JIM, *briefly considering his options before admitting*: No. It was a joke.

RON, *almost embarrassed*: Oh. Oh yeah.

JIM: But I'd be quite willing to read them – give you my opinion in a day or two.

Ron: She's right – we'll stick to plan A. (Ron *moves his suitcase to beside the back door.*) I've been a bit worried I might turn out to be one of those poor buggers who get discovered after they're dead. This is a much better scheme – being discovered after *you're* dead.

Jim: You see killing me as a career boost?

Ron: Bloody oath, mate. I'll be notorious. Publishers'll be falling over themselves to get my collected works into print. Specially if I go on the run and lead the cops a bit of a dance. (*He sighs.*)

There's the crying shame of it – means leaving the old home town.

Jim: I would have thought that was half the attraction.

Ron: Don't you say a word against Hawera, mate! No better place in the world!

Jim: Why do all your plans seem to culminate in leaving it?

Ron: If I could get world famous sitting here I wouldn't budge an inch. Sad fact of it is, if I wanna excite some attention – make a bit of a splash – gotta go bush. Sort of George Wilder – folk hero and all that. You know the caper. (*He chuckles.*)

I can see the headlines now. 'Top Poet Hung By Horse.' Christ, that'll bamboozle those university buggers! They'll be running around like headless chooks trying to fit this lot into one of their theories.

Jim: As a matter of fact, the dead horse as a symbol of academic necrophilia has been well established since Buñuel's *Chien Andalou* in the thirties.

Ron: Get away.

Jim: Those with a surrealist bent are bound to see the metaphor as somewhat obvious.

Morrieson *sucks his teeth and shakes his head.*

Ron: Nothing new under the sun, eh?

> MORRIESON *bends to the jack for the coup de grâce.*

JIM: I can only hope for a misprint. 'Top Poet Hung Like A
Horse.'

RON: Don't want my aunt finding you. I'll call the cops from
down the line – and tell them to pop round with the wagon.
They can shift the horse and all. They're always looking for
meatpacks for their raffles.
Well . . .

JIM: I wonder . . .

RON: Cheery-bye!

JIM: Perhaps – (*as things are reaching the point of no return*) –
perhaps I might have that drink now.

> MORRIESON *stops.*

RON, *suspiciously*: I thought you were a wowser?

JIM: If you had wallowed in an alcoholism as lush and green
as mine, then followed God across a dry desert plain for
fourteen years only to finish with a mouthful of ashes
– wouldn't you be feeling like getting on the piss right
now?

RON: Never let it be said that a Temperance man broke down
and asked for a drink in my house and I wouldn't give it
to him.

> *He raises the jack again, taking the pressure off* BAXTER.
> *He pulls the noose over* BAXTER's *head and helps him
> down.*

But if you think you're dodging out of this hanging – I've
got 'noose' for you. Eh? Noose for you!

> *They sit at the table.* MORRIESON *holds the shotgun loosely
> pointed at* BAXTER *as he pours the last of the whisky and
> pushes it across to him.* BAXTER *looks at it – then drinks.*

How does that feel?

JIM: A family reunion. Stiff to start off with, a little formal – then blood and love like a wave.

RON: Paddle your surfboard out – there's another one coming.

He opens a flagon and fills BAXTER'S *glass with beer.* BAXTER *drinks it down in one go.*

JIM: Like a first fuck. No, better. The first one where you know what you're doing.

RON *refills Baxter's glass and his own.*

RON: Good health.

They drink.

JIM: Have you tried *Landfall* with the short stories?

RON: Flagged it, mate. Fuck 'em.

JIM: I've found the editorial staff to consist chiefly of duck-arsed over-potty-trained pricks whose critical insight is restricted to pulling their foreskins over their heads and shouting 'I see a new national literature!' I speak charitably only because they're some of my oldest friends. (BAXTER *pours himself a drink as he relaxes into the old routine.*)

RON: See, I've got these themes in here. (*He taps his forehead.*) Majestic, like ocean liners. Life, love, death – the whole nine yards worth. But the characters – I just do 'em from life – from round here. (*He sighs.*)

Truth of it is, they're not up to all those things I want to say. They turn out – funny.

JIM: The only true characters – the fallen, the salt of the earth.

RON: Mate, you don't know how right you are. It's the little man. The character –

JIM: Trying to learn something of life in Kelburn or Remuera is like trying to twist the balls of a eunuch!

RON: You're right – and I'll tell you what. Tell you how I know.

Hawera – is the character capital of the world! Well-kept secret. Not taking any risks. You're getting your neck stretched any minute.

Hawera – Hawera has inspired my every word! Never lived anywhere else. Never wanted to! Too much going on here. Mind boggling!

He shakes his head.

Went up to Auckland once. When I was a young fella. To go to the varsity. Only been there a couple of days when I passed a house. Someone was playing the piano. Major scales. Went straight down the station and jumped the night train. Haven't budged from here since.

Aunt was the same in her day. Couldn't last the distance at Secretarial College. It's in the blood. Mother wouldn't leave the house from one week to the next. I'd take them both out for a drive on Sunday. Dressed up in their best. Pull in at the Railway Tavern for a swift half-G while they waited in the car. I wouldn't take a hundred dollars for memories like those. (*He refills their glasses.*)

Get some in! You don't have to worry about a hangover, you lucky bugger!

He laughs. BAXTER *laughs. They laugh like drains until they are both overtaken by pain and have to sit back gasping.*

You right, mate?

JIM: Heart condition.

RON: Liver. Quack reckons it looks like a dried-up bath sponge.

JIM, *groping in his pocket*: I bring little to the funeral feast. But what little I have – (*he produces a joint*) – let us share.

RON: Sad-looking rollie.

Baxter lights up.

JIM: I understand your desire for recognition – for literary success. For me ambition was the disease of middle age.

Having inhaled deeply, BAXTER *offers the joint to* MORRIESON.

RON: 'S alright, mate, I've got my Pocket Edition.

JIM, *exhaling*: But you are – in my opinion – misled.

MORRIESON sniffs the smoke curiously. He suddenly realises and jumps up in alarm.

RON: Jesus Christ! That stuff's illegal!

JIM: You're about to commit a murder.

RON: Murder's been done in Hawera!

MORRIESON checks the doors, looks out the window guiltily and pulls a curtain before returning, fascinated.

So, what's it like?

BAXTER inhales – coughs – drinks – coughs – and inhales (which fixes him). He holds the burning joint out to MORRIESON. MORRIESON *takes it and sucks gingerly.*

Can't feel anything.

JIM: At one time I thought being the best poet in the world had meaning. Then it came to me. The only important thing is people. He tangata. To help people – to care for and nurture them.

MORRIESON forgets about the joint, leaves it in his mouth and puffs on it like a normal smoke.

RON: Bloody easy for you to say. All I ever wanted was to be a proper writer. (*He muses.*) If the demons take me alive I

might even dash off something extra. 'From his maximum
security cell – *I, Assassin* by Ronald "Poet Killer" Morrieson.'
(*He pictures the scene.*)

The crush outside the court'll be terrific – 'Ron!
Ron, have the surrealists got the significance of the dead
horse right? Is it true you've made threats against Allen
Curnow?'

BAXTER's *thoughts have followed their own course, which
erupts in a fit of self-disgust.*

JIM: Caring! Nurturing! More words! More ash tapped in a tin
lid. All worthless beside a single pure action.

In India I watched a leper dying. Beside a fruit stall
under the shade of Howrah Bridge. I left him a few coins.
A fat policeman said, 'Why do you give him money now?'
The sound of those coins on his tin plate made me think of
Judas. Here Christ was coming down from his cross on the
pavement beside the fruit markets; and no one was there to
receive his body except myself and the policeman!

RON, *oblivious*: Probably bump up your sales too. All those little
poems no one read in the *Listener*.

JIM: 'Poems are trash! . . . The flesh I love will die
Desire is bafflement
But one may say that Father Noah kept
Watch while the wild beasts slept
Not knowing even if land would rise
Out of the barren waves
That ark I keep, that watch on the edge of sleep
While the dark water heaves.'

MORRIESON *fidgets.*

RON: Cripes. All that water imagery. Just gotta duck outside.

He starts to go, then remembers the shotgun. Unable to

negotiate the jacked-up horse, he pulls up a sash window and climbs out.

Hold your horses! Eh!

He disappears. BAXTER *has been sitting trancelike. His face darkens.*

JIM: I keep telling myself I'm Noah. (*He sweeps glasses and ashtray violently off the table.*) I'm not Noah! Noah built a boat that didn't leak!

I could have sat beside the dying man in the dust, taken his head on my knees and wiped his face with my handkerchief. Who am I to preach brotherhood when that is the thing I could not bring myself to do?

Why did you call me to Jerusalem? To show me I couldn't hack it! Husband, father, healer, helper – all in the dust! Nothing left! You've turned this man into an old coat and a broken stick!

Is this what you want? For me to die with all the wounds in my soul still open? Without the chance to make amends – to make myself acceptable to you!

Alright!

He climbs up and puts his head in the noose.

Damnation for this man by all means! But – what about the others? Nga mokai, the orphans? Nga raukore, the stripped and broken ones? There was a bargain. As if I said to you, 'Let my soul and body rot, let me live and die in darkness, but give these ones light, peace, joy . . .'

If my child Manu who had his head busted in the cells, and was filled full of drugs at Lake Alice – if he doesn't go into Heaven . . .

For, whoever I failed to love, I did love Manu, and put my arms round him when the death sweat was standing on

his body! If he doesn't go into Heaven, Lord Christ, then
you are not the Lord Christ!

Attracted by the noise MORRIESON *reappears at the
window.*

RON: Hoy!

BAXTER *tugs on the rope.*

JIM: Hear me!
RON: This is a murder, you bugger!
JIM: So come on then if you're coming!
RON: You're not committing suicide!

Scrambling back in, MORRIESON *dithers between* BAXTER'*s
end of the apparatus and the jack under the horse which
is looking decidedly shaky as* BAXTER *pulls on the rope
again.*

JIM: Haul away! Haul away!

MORRIESON *jumps to steady the jack but with another yank
on the rope* BAXTER *dislodges it from under the horse.*

RON: Shit!

Seeing the horse collapsing MORRIESON *throws himself
underneath. He is pinned face down by the horse's weight,
only his bottom half and waving legs showing.* BAXTER *is
pulled up onto his tiptoes, swaying dangerously on top of
the footstool. Neither is able to come to the other's aid.*

JIM: More jokes! More pratfalls! Come out from behind your
cloud for once! You've turned me into this sad old canary
that can't sing – so now knock me off my perch! I dare you!
(*He throws his arms out wide, eyes closed.*) Knock me off my
perch!

>*Suddenly the interior door behind him opens, banging into him, almost sending him flying.*

Jesus!

>*Morrieson's* AUNT*'s voice is heard.*

AUNT, *off*: Ronald?

>*The door bangs into* BAXTER *again. He teeters on the edge of falling.*

Ronald! What's wrong with this door?

>*She thrusts the door hard up against* BAXTER*. He topples and the footstool turns over.* BAXTER *just manages to grab the top of the door and cling to it, feet scrabbling for a purchase.* AUNT *pushes the door open with* BAXTER *as a passenger. She peers round the door and sees* BAXTER*, then squeezes through the gap of the door and surveys the scene.*

AUNT: Ronald!
RON, *muffled by horse*: Aunty?
AUNT: You know I don't mind you inviting your friends as long as you don't make a mess.

>AUNT *peers up at* BAXTER *who has managed to crawl up on top of the door to comparative safety. As he clings there,* BAXTER *starts to laugh, quietly at first, getting louder and more uproarious as he appreciates the joke and expresses the release he is feeling.*

RON: Sorry, Aunty.

>AUNT *sees Morrieson's suitcase. With a jolt she realises he is intending to leave Hawera – and her.*

AUNT: But Ronald – where are you going?

RON, *thinking this relates to his struggles under the horse*: Thought
    I'd try and wriggle out under his belly – but it's no go.
AUNT: Your suitcase . . .
RON: Eh? Oh! Well . . . the thing is . . .

    WILMA *is heard from outside.*

WILMA, *off*: Ron? Ron Morrieson?
RON: Oh no.

    WILMA *appears at the window with a suitcase and climbs
    in.*

WILMA: Listen, Ron—
AUNT: Miss Voot.

    WILMA *comes face to face with the* AUNT. *They both
    stiffen. The* AUNT, *seeing Wilma's suitcase, makes the
    obvious assumption that she and Morrieson are running
    away together.*

  I see.
WILMA: See what?

    The AUNT *girds her loins.*

AUNT: Ronald is indisposed. Perhaps if you came back in the
    morning?
WILMA: I won't be here in the morning.
RON, *still muffled*: You get off to bed Aunty. I've got things
    under control.
AUNT, *ignoring him and indicating Wilma's suitcase*: Are you
    taking a holiday?
WILMA: Going up north for a while? Is that what you mean?
AUNT: It was a polite enquiry.
WILMA: I'm leaving Hawera. For good.
AUNT: I see.

WILMA: So you keep saying.

AUNT, *indicating Morrieson's suitcase*: And Ronald, your suitcase?

RON: Ah. I'm lending her some luggage. I said for her to drop round and pick it up.

> AUNT *smiles with satisfaction, knowing Morrieson is lying but feeling she's foiled a scheme of Wilma's to run off with him.*

AUNT: Such a generous boy.

WILMA: He's fifty years old.

AUNT: You must have a cup of tea before you go.

RON: She's right, Aunty – I'll see to Miss Voot.

WILMA: I said some things I shouldn't've. I just wanta set things straight and get off.

AUNT: We'll clear the table and put down a cloth.

WILMA: What I've got to say is to Ron.

AUNT: I hope you don't expect me to vacate my own kitchen? (*Indicating* BAXTER.) Especially when I have a guest.

> *The two women stare at each other coolly.*

WILMA: I never expected nothing from you. Or Ron's mum. And I can't say I was ever disappointed.

You'll excuse me if I don't stay. I've got a train to catch.

> WILMA *turns back to the window and starts to climb out.*

AUNT: Leaving in your usual fashion I see.

> WILMA *stops, comes back in and puts her suitcase down.*

WILMA: You're all of you the same. You can't come straight out with anything.

AUNT: I can't think what you mean.

WILMA: You with your – manners!

AUNT: At least I have some.

WILMA: Ron with his stories all the time. Him with his poems come to that! Why can't you just say something straight out?

AUNT: I can appreciate certain standards of behaviour may seem strange to you, young lady –

WILMA: I'm not young! Not any more!

AUNT: – such as not clambering in and out of people's homes in the early hours of the morning.

WILMA: But what I am is sick! Sick to the back teeth with waiting for my life to start!

AUNT: Ronald has a life. Here.

WILMA: I'm not talking about Ron!

AUNT: He just needs to settle.

WILMA: Settle! He's been nowhere else but this backwater in fifty years!

AUNT: This is his home.

WILMA: This place is killing him! Do you think they want him here? The good, decent citizens of Hawera?

AUNT: Ronald's very highly regarded.

WILMA: Inside the walls of this house! Out there he's that larrikin Morrieson!

AUNT: No!

WILMA: The no-good booze artist who can't hold down a job –

AUNT: He's been ill!

WILMA: – who's spent his life sponging off his mother and his aunt!

AUNT: He just needs to concentrate on his guitar tuition! Start taking pupils again!

WILMA: You know what they called the two of you? Eh? You and Ron's mum?

RON: Wilma!

WILMA: The duchesses! 'There go the duchesses. Cracking on

they're something they're not.'

RON: Stop it, Wilma!

WILMA: 'Sunday drive with the alkie son!' They laugh at you!

AUNT: That's a lie!

RON: Don't you talk to her— *[like that!]*

WILMA: You're no more accepted here than Ron is! Or – (*pointing at* BAXTER) – he would be if he walked down Princes Street in broad bloody daylight! Or me! The town slut!

RON: Stop it! Stop it! Stop it!

> MORRIESON *heaves the horse off the top of him and stands, but is helpless in this storm of emotion.*

WILMA: All because I wanted to be a singer! Because I couldn't stand the boredom! Because for a few crumbs of excitement I gave more of myself than any bastard round here deserved!

> AUNT *goes to* MORRIESON *as if to claim him.*

AUNT: I just want what's best for you, Ronnie.

WILMA: Well, you've got it wrong anyway. Ron's not going anywhere.

AUNT: But—

WILMA: I'm the only one who's leaving. Me.

> *Starting to realise her mistake,* AUNT *looks at* MORRIESON *who avoids her eye but nods.*

AUNT: Alone? I don't understand.

WILMA: Don't you? Reckon it's that or end up . . .

AUNT: Like me.

WILMA: I didn't say that.

AUNT: I thought you believed in plain speaking?

WILMA: I want some kids. I want a husband. Is that so far-fetched? Asking for the moon?

> *Pause.*

AUNT: No.

WILMA: Seems like I've run through my chances here.

AUNT: You're very brave.

The two women regard each other.

WILMA: Don't feel brave.

MORRIESON – *having witnessed the collision of the two opposing poles of his life, and now their surprising rapprochement – looks stricken, torn, helpless as a sense of his own trappedness, grief and lack of bravery overwhelms him.*

AUNT: Now, we were just putting the kettle on.

WILMA: No. I don't think—

AUNT: You can't go down to that freezing station without a good cup of tea inside you. Come along, shake a leg, Ronald. (MORRIESON *doesn't move.*)
No more playing rough. Help Mr—

JIM: Baxter.

AUNT: Help Mr Baxter down.

But it's the AUNT *who assists* BAXTER *to climb down, as* MORRIESON *has turned away towards the piano and the photo of his mother.*

JIM: Terra firma. In a new country.

AUNT: Now make yourself useful, Ronald, and put the kettle on.

RON, *immobile, his back to her*: Sorry about the mess, Aunty.

AUNT: We'll clean it up in the morning.

RON, *emotional*: I just can't seem to – It's like everything's gone to hell – since . . . since . . .

AUNT *crosses to* MORRIESON *and takes his hand.*

AUNT: They were beautiful together, Mr Baxter. You've never seen such devotion.

WILMA: It's true.

AUNT: The three of us. The Three Musketeers. Ronnie's been the man of the house since he was six years old. We ran a lending library. And Ronnie's mother taught piano to keep us going.

RON: She would have given me the world. And she had a heart big enough to carry it. She wanted nothing but the best for me. The best! And how did I repay her?

AUNT: You loved her, Ronnie.

RON: By hitting the booze. By lousing up every opportunity that came my way. (*He shakes his head.*)

> I'd lie in bed some mornings, crook as a dog, and I'd hear her piano scales filling up the house. Building perfect patterns to be smashed up by some ham-fisted farm kid. And I knew she was doing it for me. Sometimes after her pupils left she'd just play. And it was like water turning into wine. I'd think, 'I'll make a go of it, ma. I swear. I'll make you proud of me.'

AUNT: Ronnie, don't you know how proud she was of you?

RON: That's what's ripping the guts out of me! (*He turns away, anguished.*) Jesus! I'm sorry, Aunty.

> AUNT *sees the state he's in and puts a hand on his shoulder.*

AUNT: Play something for us.

RON, *shaking his head*: I can't!

AUNT: She wouldn't have liked this piano standing idle. (*He resists.*) She taught you beautifully. It gave her such a thrill to hear you play.

> AUNT *seats* MORRIESON *at the piano. He hesitates for a moment, staring down at the keys, then looks up at the*

photo of his mother. He plays a classical piece with beautiful expression and increasingly obvious emotion. The music flowing from the hands of this coarse lump of a man is, as Morrieson has said himself, like water turning to wine. He plays like an angel, the eloquence of his grief filling the room like a fountain. It swells and swells until, when it's all too much, he breaks down, crying. His AUNT *holds his head and strokes him.*

AUNT: My big boy. My big boy.

As she continues to comfort MORRIESON, BAXTER, *who has watched all, speaks.*

JIM: I that was nearer thee
    Than the leaf is to the tree,
    The stone to the bedded stream
    Walk upright and alone.

WILMA, watching MORRIESON *with his* AUNT, *sees more clearly than ever where the focus of his life lies. Her chair scrapes in the silence as she stands up.*

WILMA: I . . . I won't wait for the tea.
RON: Wilma –
WILMA: I can't live in my head like you do, Ron. You look at Hawera and you see some kind of magical place – full up with things happening, and crazy people, and everything out of your stories. But I can't. Any sparkle wore off it a long time ago for me. I've gotta have something real.
    (WILMA *picks up her suitcase.*) What I came back to say – what I said – about all those years wasted . . . (*She smiles.*) I can think of worse ways to waste them.

WILMA *goes.*

AUNT, *suddenly unsure*: Miss Voot.

But Wilma is gone. AUNT *turns and looks at* MORRIESON. *The impact of Wilma's leaving on him is plain to see.* AUNT *doesn't know what to do.*

Ronnie?

RON, *strained*: The two musketeers, eh? (*He struggles not to show his misery.*) Tomorrow's Sunday. In the afternoon we could take a drive up to the cemetery.

AUNT, *lost*: I'd like that.

RON: You have a sleep in. I'll bring you breakfast in bed.

The AUNT *decides. She straightens. The strength comes back into her voice.*

AUNT: Ronald Hugh Morrieson, don't make promises you can't keep. (*She picks up his suitcase, carries it over to him and plonks it down.*) Now get along with you.

MORRIESON *looks at her, confused.*

Miss Voot's forgotten the suitcase you're lending her. You'd better take it down to the station straightaway, Ronnie. Or you'll miss her. (*She crosses the room to the door, then hesitates.*)

    If, tomorrow, something else has come up, I can take a taxi to the cemetery. I'll be alright by myself.

MORRIESON *stares at her. She turns to* BAXTER, *who is gazing at her, struck by the bravery and selflessness of her action. It's a revelation for him.*

Good night, Mr Baxter.

BAXTER *stands, presses her hand in a courtly gesture. He kisses it, then stands back.*

Look – it's almost dawn. The milking's probably started.

As she turns to the door –

RON: I love you, Aunty. You can put a ring around it.

> *They exchange a smile.* AUNT *goes. There is silence for a moment.* BAXTER *pours a drink for* MORRIESON *and places it on top of the piano.* MORRIESON *plays a scale.*

All these years. For the sound of a piano.

JIM: She's telling you you're free to go.

RON: I know what she's telling me.

> MORRIESON *stands, looks around. He holds out his hand to* BAXTER.

No offence, mate.

> *They shake.* MORRIESON *walks to the door, picks up his suitcase, looks around and exits. Pause.* BAXTER *makes his confession.*

JIM: After a day or a week of bitching
I come back always to your bread and salt.
    So you don't want my life tonight. Then what? To teach me a child's lesson. To humble me here in this house – showing me such small acts of love that will move a mountain.
    I – get you.
    The Maori say, 'The man on whom the maramatanga shines has to be the doorstep of the people.' Sometimes they might eat more of my life than they need to eat. But who am I to worry too much about that?
    My bones are taking me towards the grave. Yet still I do not know you. Still I desire to see the face of that great warrior who walked on the waters of Galilee and died on the cross. What could I say to him? 'E Ariki, taku ngakau

ki a koe' – 'Lord, my heart belongs to you'?

Lord Christ, this old pakeha doorstep is nearly worn through. But in my heart I find a small secret hope, hidden like a seed in the winter ground –

Unnoticed, MORRIESON *reappears in the doorway, and stands listening.*

– that at the moment when I die, you will reveal yourself to me – shine upon me, remove by a miracle the sins I cannot remove.

It is a small hope only. A glowworm underneath the ferns, on the edge of the cemetery. You are like the sun in the noonday sky.

E Ariki, taku ngakau ki a koe.

Silence. MORRIESON *comes back in.*

RON: Truck's fucked. (*He drops the suitcase.*) Plenty of time.

MORRIESON *tosses down the drink standing on the piano and pours himself another, trying not to show he is wavering.*

I'll hear the train. No sense freezing my bum down at the depot. (*He looks at* BAXTER.) Back on the wagon, I suppose? (*He drinks.*)

This poetry racket, mate – there any money in it? If the readies are there I reckon I could give it a burl. Tried every other bloody thing.

JIM: Why not? (*He picks up paper and pen.*) I'll take down the words.

RON: Now? Out loud?

JIM: On the tongue.

RON: What'll I write about?

JIM: Whatever comes.

MORRIESON *shapes up self-consciously to begin.*

RON: Nah – I feel like a prize dork. I've never written anything with someone in the same room.

JIM, *writing*: 'Ode to – Hawera.'

RON: Shouldn't I kick off with a tree or a vase of flowers or something?

JIM: A poet is not so much magician or dreamer. If he resembles anything it's the emu, who digests stones and old boots.

RON: I dunno, mate –

JIM, *writing*: 'I dunno, mate – '

RON: Oh, now come on . . .

JIM: 'Oh now come on . . .' I'm sending this to *Landfall* by first post. With your name on it.

RON: Right, ya bugger –

JIM: Write, you bugger.

RON: O . . . Hawera!
    Thou great . . . horse's arsehole!
        'Horse's arsehole'? That's fucked! What kind of poetry is that?

JIM: Keep going!

RON: You keep going!

JIM: Hawera – horse's arsehole
    What iron frost grips your knackers
    Out of season? . . .

RON: Just a minute, mate. If anyone's going to put the boot into this town— *[it'll be me.]*

JIM: 'Out – of – season . . .'

MORRIESON *jumps in.*

RON: Dawn cracks like an egg into your main drag
  Spilling the Rotary President butcher
  Farting and whinging out of his sister-in-law's bed

  Slowly at first, gathering momentum, the poem starts to
  roll.

An hour from now he'll be scraping mouldy bread
Into the sausage mix, parting the plastic-strip flyscreen
Of another day, conning bored pregnant wives with
        green-nosed kids
That he'd slip them some beef tea in bed
Soon as look at them – telling me pissy-eyed later on
'Mate – it's the fuckin' highlight of their day!'
Yeah, and morning breaking too on pub
And Post Office, eclipsing the blue all-night light
Of Davies Gas Station and Lubritorium
Where Jim who lost his boy in a shunting accident
Lies cold, shit-faced round a flagon of Blackberry Nip
While a quarter mile away, as still as a corpse
His wife is staring at the faded wallpaper.
Then the whistle goes at the Treatment Station
As sharp and quivering in the chilly air
As a chord on a cool vibraphone.
From the hinterland to the coast the lazy wind blows
– so lazy it'd rather go through you than round you –
As the young cop with the seven-a-side moustache
Drives through town thinking of the electrically charged
        flesh
Of a girl at a dance, and the old cop, spindle shanked
And herring gutted, unshaven as an albino hedgehog
Heaves his brewer's goitre on top of his wife with the
        bung eye.
Sadness dives and collars me low, and the sun
Supposed to disperse the chimeras of the small hours

Only serves to sheet them home. Donkey deep,
        somewhere
Down the line this town turned dog on me, its narrow
        roads
Shooting away like arrows only ever returned me here,
        waking
With a labouring heart, enough dirty water on my chest
To sink a boat. Hawera, horse's arse, from metho kings
To bible-bangers yawns and stretches, dips its lips in
        Ovaltine,
Forgets its dead in the yellow cemetery. Today
In shaking sunshine with no zip in it, I'll punch arms
And slap backs, grinning away with murder in my heart
Good old Ron, booze artist, bullshitter and headmaster
Of the most hectic school of froth-blowers in the south
Taranaki — but there's the wheel of a Leyland ten-tonner
Leaning on my heart, a six-foot trench on my trail,
The whole town chipping in for a headstone. This hard
        case
Remembers nights, the moon in the gutter of the sky
With its parking lights on, brandy glowing like a beacon
In the belly, swooping home down the back roads
From the first time a woman wrapped her legs around me
Saying 'Boy that feels good.' And home was Ma — and
        that open grave
That sits drinking with me in the Imperial leans across
        the table
To say 'Just curl up in me, son — they'll plant you where
You can lay your head on her lap like you used to as a kid
Coming back on the train from Opunake beach.' And I
        want to —
I'm tired and I want to — but instead I stagger out into the
        empty street
Where a cannonball wouldn't startle a tom cat

With my brain screaming, 'Run, boy, run!
Change the scenery – shoot through – get lost! Fuck off
Out of it and away!'
But Hawera and me – deeper than blood
A boiled carrot and a hunk of corned brisket
What can I say? – As my grave catches up with me
On the street beside the TAB, lights my smoke
And arm in arm we head on our way –
Alright
Alright! Alright!
I'll stay.

    Pause. He turns to BAXTER.

Not going too fast was I, mate?

    BAXTER *is deep asleep and has been for most of the poem.*
    MORRIESON *slips the piece of paper out of his fingers, looks*
    at the few scrawled lines and, amused, screws it up. He
    takes his coat off and puts it over BAXTER, *then moves his*
    suitcase to the inside door. As he goes to close the piano
    lid the train whistle sounds from the station. MORRIESON
    listens, fingers a scale, then sits down and plays a jaunty
    jazz tune ('Ain't Misbehavin'') as the whistle fades into
    the distance. The light brightens outside the window and
    the birds start to sing. Fade. Audio crossfade into record of
    'Ain't Misbehavin''.

    The End.

FLIPSIDE
THE MEN OF THE *ROSE-NOËLLE*

ADAPTED FROM *CAPSIZED*
BY J. NALEPKA AND S. CALLAHAN

Introduction

Rub-a-dub-dub, four men in a tub.

By the time I came to the writing of this play, the story of the *Rose-Noëlle,* and the four men who survived drifting under her upturned hull for one hundred and nineteen days, had already been told many times. Through newspapers, TV news bulletins and current affairs shows, via two books and a dramatised TV documentary. Jim Nalepka had even appeared on Oprah. So why did I want to tell the story again?

Because there was something yet to tell, or at least to dramatise, and that was the emotional story. Virtually every other account had concentrated on the physical circumstances. Sure, they'd encompassed the interpersonal frictions, but nothing, with the exception of Jim Nalepka and Steve Callahan's book *Capsized,* had actually been able to bring any great insight to the human story. The physical journey John, Jim, Rick and Phil had been on was very interesting, but their emotional journey was fascinating.

I had nursed my idea for a play about the *Rose-Noëlle,* or more accurately the men of the *Rose-Noëlle,* for a number of years before I read *Capsized.* I knew straightaway that any play would have to be an adaptation of the book – the material in it was so rich, wry, hilarious, dramatic, honest and full of insights. Jim Nalepka is an amazing man, to be able to understand his own and his companions' emotional responses and to be open and forthright about them.

I tracked Jim down via a letter which went round the world before I discovered he was in Nelson, just across Cook Strait from me. Jim's co-author Steve Callahan had also survived a similar experience at sea. Both men kindly gave me permission to adapt *Capsized* for the stage.

My first challenge was to wrestle down the wealth of

material. I still believe I could have made another full-length play from what I left out. My goal was somehow to turn the story and the characters inside out, to turn the spotlight on what they felt more than what they did. Wanting to stay away from a standard story format – and the outside-looking-in quality that entails – I decided not to work chronologically. My strategy was to seize on anything I thought useful and make a scene out of it. My first draft was a 'compost' of scenes over one hundred and fifty pages long, in no particular order and using a number of different tones and styles.

We had a reading of this and it went down well (perhaps not the best phrase for a shipwreck story). I briefly had visions of doing this pile of scenes in random order each night, again to break down the details of a by now well-known story in order to look at what lay beneath. But there was a better way to go, and that was to follow Jim through the story: to have him talk to the audience, to allow him to be the keyhole for the audience to enter emotionally what was going on. This could dramatise the essentially different take that Jim and Rick had on events, and their attempts to make sense of what had happened. Rick's deathbed, and the last day they saw each other, became the context through which events on the *Rose-Noëlle* were imparted – not as a dead-in-the-water inert narrative but as an active and last-ditch attempt to draw some meaning from it or at least change the other's point of view. The bed became the boat, and vice versa.

Scenes of the action story, which were great in themselves but didn't contribute to this spine, began to fall away as the shape of the play emerged more and more clearly. Three basic levels of performance remained – the four men interacting on the *Rose-Noëlle*, Jim and Rick wrestling with themselves and each other in Rick's bedroom, and Jim speaking directly to us. It was then a case of weaving in and out of these levels as seamlessly as possible and in an order which would make for cumulative emotional sense and power. What theatre does best in other words.

Flipside was the first – and so far the only – play I'd written with an all-male cast. It led to a more boysy than usual rehearsal process with the actors much given to farting indiscriminately while crammed together for scenes in the 'cave'. It was a pleasure for me to work on that initial Circa production with a great cast and designer (Lizz Santos, the sole woman aboard) and particularly to have Simon Bennett once again direct one of my plays.

Audience members who gazed dubiously at our bedroom set as the lights went down, wondering, 'Where was the boat? Where was the ocean?', soon found their answer. Principally they were in the soundscape, designed by Peter Edge – a world of sound and music which took us everywhere, told us where we were and incorporated everything from John Denver to a freak wave as large as our imaginations could contain. So effective was this immersion into the world of the play that during the interval (following the 'thirst' section) the audience would bolt for the water in the foyer.

Friends and family of the men from the *Rose-Noëlle* came to see *Flipside* (and, in the case of Jim Nalepka, one of the crew members himself). They were generous in their support and feedback and were impressed with how the actors (especially Tim Spite as Rick Hellriegel) had intuitively picked up physical mannerisms of the real men.

I wrote in the programme of that production: 'First of all (and here, last of all) I have to thank the crew of the *Rose-Noëlle* – John Glennie, Phillip Hofman, Rick Hellriegel and Jim Nalepka – who, though they had no intention of providing source material for a stage play, nevertheless did so with a rare combination of humour, humanity and honesty.'

First Performance

Flipside was first performed at Circa Theatre, Wellington, on 7 October 2000, with the following cast:

JOHN:	Edward Campbell
PHIL:	Tim Bartlett
JIM:	Gareth Reeves
RICK:	Tim Spite

Director	Simon Bennett
Designer	Lizz Santos
Lighting	Ash Shaham
Composed by	Peter Edge
Stage Manager/Operator	Shane Bosher
Publicity/Production Manager	Heidi Simmonds
Production Photography	Stephen A'Court
Poster Photography	Matt Grace
Set Construction	B&P Engineering
	Hal Martin
Graphic Design	Dougal MacPherson
House Manager	Suzanne Blackburn
Front of House	Linda Wilson

Characters

JOHN: 48
PHIL: 42
JIM: 38
RICK: 31

JOHN, PHIL and RICK are New Zealanders, JIM is American.

Setting

A bed and bedroom that do equal duty as boat, cabin and everything else. The soundscape is particularly important in seguing between different environments. Actors mime or adapt props where necessary.

Act One

Darkness. Distant sounds of a storm at sea. A dim light comes up slowly to reveal RICK *propped up in bed, dozing. Another light reveals* JIM *standing at the front of the stage. He has a packed bag beside him and another bag slung over his shoulder. He speaks out to the audience.*

JIM: All our time together on the *Rose-Noëlle*, one thing never changed. John and Phil shared a blanket, but Rick and I had the sleeping bag – our feet together in the tapered pocket at the bottom, the wide flap at the top arranged across our shoulders. When things were bad we'd find each other's hand and hold on. I'd feel the warmth of Rick's body – and its fragility. Feel pity for him, and gentleness. And know that I also was worthy of pity and gentleness.

The storm sounds rise as RICK *begins to dream. Snatches of voices are tossed on the wind –*

PHIL, *voice-over*: It's got to be blowing forty knots out there! It's getting worse!

JIM, *voice-over*: Rick, are we OK?

RICK, *voice-over*: John – lash the helm and get down here!

JIM, *voice-over*: Can he hear you?

JOHN, *voice-over*: We're fine. It's just another blow . . .

PHIL, *voice-over*: Can anyone hear me? This is the *Rose-Noëlle*. (*Mutating into radio.*) The *Rose-Noëlle*. Over . . .

During this JIM *has picked up the bag beside him and entered Rick's room. Seeing him asleep,* JIM *puts both bags down, stacking them both out of Rick's line of sight. He stands looking at* RICK *for a moment before moving to the side of the bed.*

JIM: Rick . . . (RICK *doesn't move. The sound of the storm swoops to its loudest yet.*) Rick?

As JIM *reaches out and touches* RICK's *hand – boom! A huge wave smashes into the boat and* JIM *and we are pitched headlong into* RICK's *dream.*

PHIL, *scrambling up*: It's got to be blowing forty knots out there!

> RICK, JIM *and* PHIL *are in the cabin.* JOHN *is at the helm.* JIM *grabs onto* RICK *to steady himself.*

JIM: Rick, are we OK?
PHIL, *panicking*: It's getting worse!
RICK, *to* JIM: Yeah – we're OK.
PHIL: Never underestimate the power of water! The sea takes no prisoners.
JIM: Thanks, Phil.

> *Boom! The boat is hit and rocked by another huge wave.* PHIL *jumps up in his berth and hits his head on the ceiling.*

PHIL: Ah!
RICK, *calling up to* JOHN *at the helm*: John – lash the helm and get down here!

> JOHN *is oblivious.*

JIM: Can he hear you?

> RICK *shrugs.*

PHIL: I've got to get out of here!
JIM: What if John gets swept overboard – what do we do then?
RICK, *going to the ladder again*: For Christ's sake, John!

He is almost flattened as JOHN *drops down into the cabin.*
He shakes frigid water off himself.

What's the story, John?
JIM: What do we do now?
PHIL: Let's get on the radio – tell someone what's going on!
JOHN, *unperturbed*: Ah, nice cup of tea. Lovely.

JOHN *ignores them, pouring himself a cup of tea.*

RICK: How bad is it going to get?
JIM: How long's this going to last?
PHIL: How big a wave will it take to flip us?

JOHN *concentrates on his tea, with a smirk of amusement*
at his crew's fears.

JOHN: Look. This boat will never capsize. It can't capsize.
JIM: Even in this?
JOHN: I've sailed forty thousand miles and this is just another
    blow.

Boom! Everyone is rattled and shaken out of the dream state, RICK
falls back across the bed. As the storm recedes and the lights revert
to bedroom –

JIM: Rick . . . ?

JIM, *his hand on* RICK'S *wrist, gently shakes him. As* RICK
stirs –

RICK: Still here, mate . . .

– the last of the storm sounds abate and disappear. JIM
passes a drink with a straw. RICK *takes a sip and leans*
back. His right side is partially paralysed, arm and leg

useless, right eye and that side of his mouth drooping, speech a little slurred.

Get everything organised?

JIM, *nodding*: All set. (*There's an awkward pause – which* JIM *deflects with –*) Guess who I bumped into in town? Phil.

RICK: Yeah?

JIM: He's stacked it back on. You should see him. The old teddy bear he was. Good for snuggling up to on cold nights.

RICK: And cold days.

JIM: Yeah.

RICK: 'Cept for his toenails.

JIM: And his wispy hair tickling you.

RICK: And his titanic belches.

JIM: Can't do that now. He'd wake the baby.

RICK: Philippa Rose.

He shakes his head, and grins lopsidedly. JIM *smiles too.*

JIM: Phil 'The Hook' Hofman. Remember how when we called him that he'd puff his chest out?

RICK: Strutting up and down with the gaff –

JIM: What about that time he was out on the hull, clothes off, getting some sun, and that big kingfish just jumped right out of the water onto the hull beside him?

RICK: Thought his eyes were going to bug out on stalks –

They're both laughing as they remember.

JIM: And how he dived on it –

Laughing, JIM *mimes the chase of* PHIL *trying to catch the slippery fish in a bear hug which it shoots out of repeatedly.*

RICK, *crying with laughter*: With his . . . his white arse –

JIM: – winking at us!

RICK's *laughter stops as he's grabbed by pain.*

OK?

RICK *nods, grimacing. He rides it out.* JIM *rearranges the pillows behind him.*

Can I get you anything?

RICK, *nodding*: Get me out of here. (JIM *smiles ruefully.*) I just wish I was going with you.

JIM: Me too, Rick. Me too.

RICK: Like to see the look on everyone's face – if I just got out of this bed – and walked out.

JIM: Yeah!

RICK: Off on another adventure.

JIM: Just do it.

RICK: You reckon?

JIM: That's what you told me. That morning in the kitchen at Anakiwa.

RICK: Me? Nah.

JIM: Sure. Once you'd finished gloating.

Sound: Large kitchen. JIM *is busy. Reverting to his 'well' self,* RICK *barges in.*

RICK: Coffee on?

JIM, *busying himself*: Coffee's on – a hundred-egg omelette is cooked and eaten – thirty loaves of bread have become toast and disappeared – and ten gallons of porridge is now setting like concrete in the intestines of a hundred traumatised Outward Bounders.

RICK: Anything to eat? (*He finds something and consumes it heartily.*)

JIM: They might be having a kind of fake adventure out there – but at least it's something. Did I come halfway across the

world just to cook breakfast for everyone else?
RICK, *mouth full*: Buggered if I know, mate – I'm off to Tonga.
JIM: Tonga?
RICK: Sailing to Tonga. Crewing on a yacht. Catch ya. (*He goes.*)
JIM: The Islands. Wow!

> RICK *comes back, grabs* JIM *and grins.*

RICK:What d'ya reckon, Jim? Fancy going to Tonga?
JIM: You're kidding.
RICK: Skipper needs one more on the crew.
JIM: I've never sailed before.
RICK: Come on, mate.
JIM: I dunno, Rick.
RICK: Just do it!

Reverting to bedroom –

JIM: See?
RICK: Bloody stupid advice. What'd ya want to listen to me
    for?
JIM: Beats me, Rick.
RICK, *grinning*: You wouldn't have missed it. You didn't want
    me floating around out there all by myself did you?
JIM: You wouldn't have been all by yourself. You'd have had Phil
    for company, – (RICK *snorts.*) – and John.
RICK, *grunting*: Dickhead.

> *Pause.*

JIM: Rick, you know how after we got off the *Rose-Noëlle* I asked
    you if you felt humbled? And you said—
RICK: Shit no!
JIM: You still feel like that?
RICK, *shrugging*: I guess so. What was there to be humbled
    about?

JIM: Don't you ever ask yourself what the meaning of it was?

RICK: 'Meaning'?

JIM: Why it happened.

RICK: We know *why* it happened. Because our captain was a
    fuckwit – that's why!

JIM: That's not completely true, Rick.

RICK: Right from the off! That thing with the ferry.

JIM: I know.

RICK: Before we'd even got out of Cook Strait – remember?

JIM: I remember you just before, up at the helm with the wind
    in your hair. 'God I've needed this.'

RICK: Bullshit.

JIM: True! Right on nightfall . . .

Sound: Rose-Noëlle *under sail –*

JIM, *out*: Rick doing the steering. John and Phil shaking out
    extra sail to put more speed on. And me busy – untying
    my shoe. And tying it up again. 'Cos I don't know what the
    hell to do on this boat, and everyone else does.

RICK: God, I've needed this. Nothing but open water between
    us and Tonga.

JIM, *coming up behind him – kid's voice*: How far now, Dad?

> *They laugh.* RICK *demonstrates.*

RICK: See, Jim? You just keep her straight down the face of the
    wave.

> JIM *nods. He glances back and sees something.*

JIM: Hey Rick – what's that?

> RICK *checks behind then calls forward.*

RICK: John, the ferry's behind us.

JOHN *doesn't turn or react. He keeps working on the sails with* PHIL.

JIM: It's kinda windy. I don't know if he heard you. (JIM *looks back.*) Boy, it's really moving.

RICK *looks back again, then forward.*

RICK: John – you seen this ferry?

JOHN *doesn't react.*

JIM: Look at the size of it.

Rattled, both RICK *and* JIM *call forward.*

RICK: John!
JIM: John!

JOHN *doesn't turn, but beside him* PHIL's *eyes are now fixed on the ferry as well.*

PHIL: Hey mate, do ya see the ferry?
JOHN: Yep.
JIM, *to* RICK: Do you think *it* can see *us*?
RICK, *suddenly realising*: John! Are the bloody mast lights on?

Everyone's heart lurches, but JOHN's. *He casually but nimbly lopes back, drops into the cockpit and flips a switch.* RICK's *still holding the wheel but* JOHN *pulls down on it so the* Rose-Noëlle *veers away slightly.* JIM, RICK *and* PHIL *stare upwards big-eyed as the ferry slides past like a glacier.* JOHN *laughs, obviously amused by the others' anxiety. They turn to look at him.*

JOHN: That was my good old buddy Brownie up at the helm. He wouldn't have hit us.

As he moves off grinning, the others continue to stare at him. The 'at sea' soundscape drops for a couple of lines –

RICK: We should've jumped overboard and swum for the ferry right there and then.

JIM: Rick, I can't swim that well. Besides, you were enjoying yourself. So was I even.

– before coming back up as JIM *pulls his balaclava down and grasps the wheel to take his turn on watch. He repeats his instructions.*

'Straight down the face of the wave.' (*Tentative at first,* JIM *starts to relax.*) Alright! It's just like driving a car really. Except you can't wind the window up.

The Rose-Noëlle *plunges forward down a long wave –*

Woah!

– and hitting the bottom at the wrong angle, slews violently sideways with a jarring wrench. JIM *over-corrects one way, then the other, wrestling with the wheel.* JOHN *pops up like a jack-in-the-box, pushes* JIM *aside and corrects their course.*

JOHN: Don't you know how to steer a boat?

JIM, *crushed, and a bit nervous*: Waves are getting kind of big aren't they John?

JOHN: These latitudes you can get forty-footers.

JIM *tries to imagine that – with more success than he would like – as* JOHN *looks round with satisfaction.*

There's a storm coming up from the Antarctic.

JIM: Do you think we can outrun it?

JOHN: Outrun it? We're going to catch it! It'll blow us up to

Tonga in no time flat. Steady as you go.

> JOHN *leaves* JIM *to it.* JIM *now stands rigidly, muscles clenched from his jaw to his fingers as he grips the wheel, afraid to relax or take a hand off.*

JIM: Oh no – itchy balaclava.

> JIM *tries to ignore it and squirms. He removes one hand from the wheel to try to slip the balaclava off. He gets it stuck over his eyes, struggles, and has to use both hands. By the time he frees himself the boat is going broadside to the waves. As* JIM *reaches for the wheel, the* Rose-Noëlle *bucks with a sickening lurch, throwing* JIM *to the other end of the cockpit. As he fights his way towards the wheel which is spinning out of control,* JOHN *bounds up from below, annoyed.*

JOHN: You really don't know how to steer a boat!

> JOHN *wrestles the boat back on to course and stands at the wheel, ignoring* JIM *who slumps down disconsolately. After a moment* RICK *comes up to relieve the situation.*

RICK: It's OK, John – I'll take the wheel.

> JOHN *nods, makes way for* RICK *and heads below.* JIM *looks at* RICK *gratefully.*

JIM: Thanks Rick, I know it's not your watch for another hour.
RICK: No worries, mate. You'll get the hang of it in no time.
JIM: Not off John. He doesn't seem to want to explain anything.
RICK: Just watch me. (*He takes a cassette out.*) And put some music on.

> JIM *plugs it in and Bo Diddley's 'I'm a Man' plays.* JIM *starts to relax and enjoy himself as he and* RICK *boogie*

along, sliding down the waves in a rush of exhilaration.

Tonga, here we come!

JIM: Everyone at Outward Bound can eat their heart out! We're on a real adventure!

Boom! Cross to –

Sound: Storm. The four of them are in the cabin after JOHN *has lashed the helm. Boom!* PHIL *springs up and bumps his head again.*

PHIL: Ah! We're going too fast, John!

JOHN: We're fine. The helm's lashed.

PHIL: We're out of control!

JOHN: I told you, it's just another blow.

PHIL: We need to get that sea anchor out!

> JOHN *is unmoved.* PHIL *appeals to* RICK.

Rick?

RICK: I agree with Phil. It'll stabilise us – make sure we stay head-on into the weather.

JIM, *clutching a bucket and weighing in a little timidly*: Sounds like a good idea to me.

> JIM *retches.* JOHN *looks at his sorry crew, then slaps his hand down decisively and gets to his feet.*

JOHN: OK. Who's going out there with me?

> *As* JOHN *struggles into his sodden wet weather gear,* JIM *and* PHIL *are shamefaced, but scared rigid at the thought of going out into the storm raging outside.* RICK *rises.*

RICK: I'll go, mate. (*It's not clear whether he's talking to* JOHN *or to* JIM.)

As RICK *makes to follow* JOHN *up on deck, 'I'm a Man' continues to play ironically.* JIM *and* PHIL *glance at each other, and look away.*

Storm sounds fade as the scene reverts to the bedroom. RICK *is back in the bed.*

JIM: You've gotta give him that much, Rick. John put the parachute out – even though he didn't want to – just to please us.

RICK: We shouldn't have had to beg him to do it! Any halfway decent skipper would have had it out already.

JIM: A lot of the time, Rick, you just dismissed whatever John said.

RICK: After we turned over! After he turned out to be full of it!

JIM: I know – and sometimes I was as down on him as you. But you didn't hear him talk like I did. Even before we left Picton.

Sound: Marina, dockside –

JOHN: Just get me back to the Islands, Jim. The swinging sixties weren't London for me. They were thirty-five thousand miles of ocean. My brother David and I bouncing around the South Pacific – from San Francisco to French Polynesia. If you're going to San Francisco wear some flowers in your hair. They've been doing that in Tahiti for a thousand years. Women treat you right there. And they're beautiful. Like Rose-Noëlle.

JIM, *patting the boat*: This *Rose-Noëlle*?

JOHN: Rose-Noëlle Coguiec. Miss Tahiti of 1968. Are you storing those walnuts, Phillip, or eating them?

PHIL, *mouth full of walnuts*: Righto, John.

JIM: Does Miss Tahiti know you named your boat after her?

JOHN: Perhaps. She died in a plane crash at Papeete Airport in '73. Still young, still beautiful. I like to think she knows – and that she'll take care of me. (*He raps on the hull with his knuckles.*) She's a dream, Jim. An Airex PVC foam sandwich core, laminated on both sides with fibreglass – and my only home. Everything I know about boat building's in her. All my money, time, skill – even love. Especially love.

JIM: The Islands sound great. You haven't been back?

JOHN, *shaking his head*: Nineteen years since that voyage with my brother – making our names as playboys of the South Pacific. That's the title of the book I wrote about it – Playboys of the South Pacific. Almost got it published too. But it was turned down by a woman editor. You know how they are.

Nineteen years. You get on land and you get stuck, Jim. Just get me back there.

Boom! Cross to storm –

PHIL *jumps up in his berth and bangs his head.*

PHIL: Ah!

JOHN, *from in the galley*: Taking you to the Islands is going to be good for you, Phillip. Never been out of the country – at your age!

PHIL *agitatedly peers out at the storm continuing to rise outside.*

PHIL: I don't like it, John. I really don't like it.

JOHN *turns from the galley with plates of food.*

JOHN: Here – eggs and chilli. Get this into you.

RICK and JIM *look at the mess on their plates queasily.*

JIM: For how long?

PHIL is oblivious to anything but his rising panic as he buttonholes JOHN.

PHIL: We've gotta tell someone we're out here!
JOHN: No, Phillip! We're fine. Now calm down and eat something.

Crash! Everything and everyone becomes airborne as Rose-Noëlle *bucks, leaps and wrenches round broadside.*

PHIL: Bloody hell!
JIM: What was that?

JOHN looks at them. Whatever he's thinking doesn't show.

JOHN: Sea anchor. Better take a look.

As JOHN *readies himself to go outside,* RICK *glances at* JIM.

RICK: You want to give it a burl this time, mate?

JIM looks everywhere but at RICK. *He tries to rouse himself, but the rattling, shrieking storm that redoubles outside conspires to strip him of any nerve he can scrape up. Seconds pass.* RICK *gets up and follows* JOHN. JIM *starts to mechanically clean up the jumbled mess in the cabin.*

PHIL: We're going to flip. I know it. That's what's going to happen. We're going to flip. (*He grabs the VHF radio.*) Can anyone hear me? This is the *Rose-Noëlle*. The *Rose-Noëlle*. Over.

He waits but there is no reply. He calls again.

Can anyone hear? Is there anyone out there?

JOHN *bursts back in, followed by* RICK. JOHN *looks at* PHIL.

JOHN: That radio's short range. The only thing you'd pick up would be a passing ship, and that's not too likely out here.

PHIL *hangs the mike back up in disgust.*

PHIL: Bloody hell, John! You've got a ham radio – tune that in!

JOHN, *chuckling*: That's only for emergencies. And this is not an emergency.

RICK, *worried by what they've seen on deck*: We've got to get out there and sort the sea anchor.

JIM: What's happened to it?

RICK: It's fouled.

JOHN: Release lines've probably tangled themselves round it.

RICK: It's pulling us round side-on to the waves. We have to get rid of it.

JOHN, *shaking his head*: Too dangerous. If we make a mistake trying to pull it in, it could take off a finger, even a hand.

RICK: Then just cut it free.

JOHN: Do you know how much that thing cost? I've only just got it.

RICK: That's hardly the point if we go over.

JOHN: We can ride this out. This boat is built to take anything. And it's too dangerous up on deck at the moment.

RICK, *looking at him a moment*: OK John, you're the skipper.

PHIL: I've had enough of this! I want you to get on that ham radio and get a helicopter, John! I want a helicopter and I want it now!

JOHN, *almost amused by Phil's state*: Take a look outside, Phillip. What's a helicopter going to do out here?

PHIL: Well, tell the coast watch we're here! Tell anyone!

JOHN: I haven't got a ham radio licence. I'm not putting myself in the gun for a fine without a damn good reason.

PHIL: But we're going to flip!

JOHN: We're *not* going to flip. This boat will never, never flip.
(*He looks round them.*)
    Everyone relax. We're fine here. We'll just sit it out.
(*He turns to a box of cassette tapes.*) I've got just the thing
here to take your mind off the weather . . .

> *He sticks in a tape of Kevin Bloody Wilson – which as*
> JIM *speaks segues into a series of sound bites from* JOHN's
> *New Age tape, BBC reports from Tiananmen Square,*
> *'Annie's Song' by John Denver, back to Kevin Bloody*
> *Wilson and round and round, speeding up till it churns*
> *into a nauseating hurdy-gurdy of sound. The music is*
> *accompanied by the rattling and banging of dishes within*
> *the cabin and booming and juddering from without as the*
> Rose-Noëlle *bounces sideways as if on a corrugated dirt*
> *road, and by* PHIL's *increasingly frenzied cries that he can't*
> *take any more, get him out of there, never underestimate*
> *the power of water, and that they're going to flip.*

JIM *comes forward.*

JIM: Kevin Bloody Wilson. John seemed to think it was
screamingly funny. If it wasn't that, it was some weird
New Age tape. I couldn't figure the guy out – jokes about
women's tits one minute, 'finding the God within' the
next. After that we turned on the radio – the BBC was
broadcasting from China where tanks were busy running
over students in Tiananmen Square. Then a sappy John
Denver love song, then more Kevin Bloody Wilson – and
all the time Phil Bloody Hofman keeping up a running
commentary of doom. And round and round – exhaustion,
sickness, smell of vomit, eggs, grease, fear, student protests,
Phil's protests, fill up my senses but do you fuck on the first
date – all coming too fast, too much, like some sort of drug

trip you can't get off, until I knew completely and utterly I couldn't take one – second – more!

Sudden silence.

Just before morning – the dishes stopped rattling in the sink. Waves weren't hitting us like a sideways jackhammer any more. They lost their white peaks and eroded into rolling hills, high and steep but rounded. The wind was still high, but the scream it had made through the generator settled back. After what we'd been through, it was like silence. As the movement became measured, my body adapted, muscles relaxed, a little peace seemed to rise up through me. I slept in the troughs of the waves, a minute here, a minute there. Even Phil was quiet.

JOHN *gets up.* RICK *looks at him for a moment.*

RICK: So today we can go sailing again?

JOHN *nods.*

A sound comes. Rising swiftly from nothing to a massive unstoppable force, rushing rapidly from far away to up very close. All four men stop and raise their heads, listening. Time hesitates as the wave towers above them. There is no time for fright. There is no doubt as to what is about to happen. Blackout.

Silence. In the darkness –

RICK: I should have grabbed a knife, gone up on deck and cut the lines to the sea anchor. Simple as that.

JOHN: Hard to say whether anything would have made a difference.

RICK: I knew it was the right thing to do – a child would have
   known!
JOHN: It was a rogue wave – a monster.
RICK: But I listened to Captain John Glennie: 'This boat will
   never ever flip.' Jesus!

*Storm sounds return – muted, dulled by the cavelike hull – water
flooding in. Lights up to illuminate, dimly, the* Rose-Noëlle
capsized, crew scattered.

RICK: Jim?
PHIL: I'm stuck! I can't move!
RICK: Jim?
PHIL: There's water coming in!
JIM, *stunned, feeling beneath him*: This is the ceiling . . .
RICK: Jim?
JIM: Here. (*They find each other in the half-dark and clasp hands.*)
   We're upside down!
PHIL: Jesus Christ, get me out of here! I'm gonna drown!
JIM: Phil, come on. This way!

> *They help* PHIL *to extricate himself from where he is
> trapped in his upside-down berth, desperation giving him
> suppleness.*

PHIL: We're in it now. We're bloody doomed.
JIM: How high's the water going to rise, Rick?
RICK: I don't know, mate.

> JOHN, *who has been stunned by the turn of events, now
> sloshes towards them.*

JOHN: Is everyone OK? The water level'll stop rising in a minute
   – when it equalises with outside. We won't sink.

JIM *breathes out with relief.* RICK *mutters.*

RICK: What a bullshit artist.

JOHN: Scoop up everything loose and pass it to me. I'll stow it in the aft cabin. We'll try to build up a base high enough so we can lie on top, out of the water. (*He stops, watching something float by.*) There's stuff floating out of here. Out of the boat. (*He turns and looks.*) The companionway doors are smashed out. Phillip – you kicked them out!

PHIL: No!

JOHN: Don't you understand, the surge will carry everything out of here! We'll have nothing left!

PHIL: I didn't!

JOHN: Jim, get down in the hatchway. Grab anything you can before it goes out.

They set to work.

JIM, *out*: The cold water up to my chest is numbing. I can feel stuff bumping against my legs as it's sucked past. I'm too slow to catch it. Jars of peanut butter, emergency flares, my kitbag full of stuff – anything and everything loose – like a vacuum cleaner hoovering out the inside of the cabin.

Ah! Got something! (*He fishes up a cassette tape.*) Kevin Bloody Wilson . . .

He flips it over his shoulder where it's consigned to the deep. JOHN *is busy packing stuff into the aft cabin as* RICK *and* PHIL *hand it to him.*

JOHN: Right – that's as good as we're going to get it for now.

PHIL: I can't get in there – I'm claustrophobic!

RICK: Suit yourself.

He scrambles in, then a shivering JIM, *followed by* JOHN. PHIL *follows, causing some squashing and much readjustment before they settle, curled into each other like spoons.*

RICK: Wet and cold.

JIM: On top of this lumpy bumpy excuse for a mattress.

RICK: Always someone's elbow or knee in your back.

JIM: I can't believe I slept. (*He closes his eyes.*)

Lights brighten. Another day –

PHIL: Turning.

> *They all turn over in unison.*

JIM: The aft cabin – our cave – the further away from the hatch you were the more stifled and cramped you felt.

RICK: Give me some air!

> *They shuffle about to create a tiny draught which* RICK *gulps in.*

PHIL: Settle down.

RICK: You settle down! It's time you took a turn on this end!

PHIL: I told you – I'm claustrophobic. I couldn't stand it!

RICK: You just want to be beside the hatch if we flip rightside up. You know whoever's over here doesn't stand a chance!

> *Sound: Wave slop and splash.*

PHIL/JOHN: Aaah!

> PHIL *and* JOHN *freeze (literally and figuratively).* JIM *and* RICK *smirk.*

JIM: That was the one drawback to being by the hatch.

RICK: When the slop inside the hull came up and smacked you with a freezing shower.

PHIL: Shit!

JOHN: Oh, my, my!

Pause.

JIM: If we go rightside up, how long do you reckon we've got to get out of here?

RICK: In the dark, underwater, with all these layers of packing and mattressing on top of us . . .

They contemplate that.

JOHN: Relax.

RICK: What d'ya mean 'relax'?

JOHN, *authoritatively*: There's no way this boat is ever going to flip rightside up again.

They all turn to stare at him.

RICK: Shuffle!

They squirm round to allow JOHN *and* RICK *to swap places. They collapse again, staring upwards in their own private thoughts.*

JIM: Ceiling patrol. Ninety per cent of my time spent staring at the ceiling. One and a half feet from my nose. You just let your eyes go unfocused – and drift off in the blur.

Sometimes the noise of doors and hatches banging – stuff knocking around in the wash inside the hull – turns into other things. Bits of conversation. A radio. The sound of traffic.

Slowly you come back in – focus on the ceiling – the little bumps and marks you use to check if anyone's taking any of your space.

RICK nudges JIM. They exchange a mischievous glance, then subtly expand their centre space, sprawling out more expansively. JOHN and PHIL are aware straightaway that they're being pushed further into and up the walls on their respective sides.

JOHN: Well, I don't know what's going on – but suddenly I haven't got enough room.

> RICK *and* JIM *smirk at each other, enjoying the game.*

PHIL: Yeah, what's going on?

RICK, *suppressing a laugh*: It's not us, mate.

PHIL: John?

JOHN: I'm halfway up the wall here.

PHIL, *trying to spread out*: Come on, give a man some space here . . .

RICK, *resisting – mostly out of bloody-mindedness*: Show me a man, and I'll give him some.

> PHIL *snaps, and rolls over.*

PHIL, *jabbing his finger into* RICK's *chest*: Get outa my space!

> RICK *responds in kind, face blazing with anger, nose to nose with* PHIL.

RICK: Don't you poke your finger at me! Ever!

> *They glare at each other.* JIM *puts his hand on* RICK's *arm.*

JIM: Rick . . .

> PHIL *rolls back over,* RICK *drops back down. Everyone feels worse than before. Silence.*

John?

JOHN: Hmm?

JIM: Where are we going?

JOHN, *looking at him a moment*: Sure you want to know?

JIM, *knowing this can't mean anything good, but nodding*: Yeah.

> JOHN *reaches up to one of the lockers and pulls out a chart.*

He unrolls it on his own chest in the confined space.

JOHN: This is where we were. (*He points to New Zealand on one side of the chart.*) We're probably round about here now. (*He moves his finger about an inch and a half out into the ocean.*) Drifting in this direction.

JIM, *dismayed, looking at the chart*: But there's nothing there. Nothing until – (*his hand roams across the chart to the outline of coast on the other side*) – South America . . .

Everyone contemplates this.

How far is that?

JOHN, *shrugging*: Five thousand miles.

JIM: How fast do you think we're drifting?

JOHN, *shrugging again, hard to say*: Ten . . . twenty miles a day.

JIM: But that'd take – (*he does swift calculation*) – at least eight months! We'd have to float all the way to Chile!

JOHN: Well . . .

JIM: Well what?

JOHN: Can't see us making landfall in Chile. The current would catch us while we were still well out to sea, sweep us north up the line of the continent.

JIM: How far?

JOHN, *shrugging*: Another thousand miles. Maybe more.

RICK: Great. I've always wanted to go to Ecuador.

Pause.

PHIL, *morbid*: Read about this ship once. Left New Zealand in 1890. Disappeared. Turned up derelict, rotten – still afloat – off the coast of Chile. In 1915. Twenty-five years later.

Just what they all wanted to think about. Thanks, Phil.

RICK: How was the crew? In good spirits?

Despite themselves they laugh. Until a wave comes up and smacks PHIL *and* RICK.

RICK/PHIL: Aaahh! Shit!

Sound reverts to bedroom. RICK'*s left hand is covering his right eye and side of his face.*

JIM: OK, Rick?

RICK: There's some light – between the curtain . . . (JIM *crosses to twitch the curtain fully closed.*) It's like a knife.

JIM: Can I get you a drink, Rick?

> RICK *shakes his head.*

> You want me to read to you? (RICK *shakes his head again.*) Won't be long till Heather gets here.

> *Pause.*

RICK: Seems a long time ago we sat on that keel. And promised each other—

JIM, *guilty*: Don't remind me of that, Rick. Not today.

> RICK *reaches out and grasps* JIM'*s hand. They hold on.* RICK *fights to control his emotion,* JIM *too.*

You know, there were lots of times – when things were bad, and you'd find my hand and hold it. I'd feel like without you there . . . I'd die. (*Unable to speak,* RICK *nods to say 'me too'.*) Maybe it's crazy to just walk out now. It's not too late to call the whole trip off.

RICK: Don't be stupid.

JIM: What's the big deal about writing a book?

RICK: Ask John Glennie. He's already done it for you.

> JIM *looks at him, picking up the trace of protest.*

JIM: Yeah, but not the way I want to, Rick.

RICK, *nodding*: I sure don't want his version being the only one out there.

JIM: It's just – this guy who's going to help me write it – he's expecting me, he's put aside the time. And my sister hasn't seen me in—

RICK, *cutting across*: You go. Come back and tell me all about it.

> JIM *doesn't voice what he's thinking – that* RICK *won't be here by the time he gets back.*

Eh?

JIM: Yeah. I'll tell you all about it.

RICK: Meet someone over there. Bring her back. Martha wasn't right for you – running out on you like that . . .

JIM: That wasn't her fault, Rick.

RICK: We get off the boat and she's already got her tickets booked back to Canada.

JIM: She thought I was dead. That we were all dead. She'd already grieved and moved on.

RICK: In four months!

JIM: How do you think I felt about it, Rick?

> *Pause.*

RICK: I don't know, mate. I never really knew.

JIM, *looking at* RICK: All that time I dreamed about getting back to her, made up every kind of passionate scene, imagined the intimacy. But as much as I wanted it to be, as much as Martha wanted it to be . . .

It'd been tough on her too, Rick. No word, no one to support her but Heather. She needed looking after as much as I did. But I had nothing to give to her. I was all out. I felt like a dead man back in her life, asking her to warm me up.

Besides – I couldn't help but compare.

RICK: Compare?

JIM: To how you and Heather are. You know, I still think about those letters you wrote to Heather while we were out there. The things you said – even the look on your face now when it's change of shift and you know she's coming.

RICK: What . . . ?

JIM: You get excited, Rick – you're like a schoolboy.

RICK: Yeah, well . . .

JIM: That's what I wanted. Something like the two of you have got. And I guess I always knew me and Martha weren't that.

> RICK *shakes his head.*

RICK: Funny how you read those letters to Heather, and she never did get to see them.

JIM: Did you tell her the things that you wrote?

RICK: I tried, mate. But – like you said – I guess it's just different. How you think it'll be when you get back, and how it really is.

> As RICK *moves he inadvertently touches 'The Bear' –* PHIL's *wet wadded-up sheepskin coat – and recoils.*

RICK: Ugh! When are you going to dump this soaking lump of leather over the side, Phil?

Sound: Back on the boat. Creak and groan as Rose-Noëlle *rises and falls –*

PHIL: That's a good coat, mate. My brother-in-law gave me it. Gonna try to dry it out when the weather's better.

JOHN, *writing in his notebook*: Wind's dying down now.

RICK: Great. Now we've got the hole cut through to the top,

today we need to get out on the hull and jury-rig a mast.
We've got that spar we can jam in the keel. Then John you
could dive into the outriggers – see about those spare sails.

JOHN: I've told you – even if you could raise a sail we're too low
in the water to be navigable.

RICK: Yeah, you told me John – but I'd like to see for myself.

JOHN: It's wasted energy.

RICK: According to who?

JOHN: This boat is seventy per cent underwater. You can't sail it.

RICK: How do you know till you try?

JOHN: I know.

RICK: I'm suggesting something! At least it's a plan, something
towards getting us out of here! What's your idea? That we
just sit here?

JOHN: Exactly.

RICK: Oh, for fuck's sake!

JOHN: I don't see any of you diving into the hull. But every day
there's something more you want me to scrounge up.

JIM: Come on, John, you know where everything is.

JOHN: It takes me hours to warm up afterwards. It's taking it
out of me.

JIM: We realise that, John . . .

RICK: Yeah well, whose fault— *[is that in the first place?]*

JOHN, *overriding*: Now you want me to dive underneath the
boat – into the outriggers. What if I get tangled in the
rigging under there? What if I'm hurt, or any of us, from
some crackpot attempt to sail? If anything happens to us
we've got nothing out here to fix ourselves up with.

PHIL: You're right there, mate. But Rick's got a point –

JOHN: There's food squirrelled away all over. We've got a hundred
and fifty litres of water in the tanks. The best thing we can
do is sit tight, conserve energy, keep ourselves healthy. And
that means not taking stupid risks.

RICK: Who are you calling stupid?

JOHN: We're in the Southern Ocean, deep water. No matter how important you think you are in the world, it's all the same out here. We're not in control any more – and we just have to accept that.

RICK: Bullshit! (*He leans forward, vehement, speaking for all their benefit.*) I'll tell you something. Three years ago the doctors found a tumour – (*points to his head*) – right here. They gave me a sixty per cent chance of surviving another two Christmases. I should have got them to put some money on it. Twenty-five radiation treatments and that thing was zapped, fried, gone. And you want to know why? Because not once did I give in to it. Not once did I believe I was going to die. You can say it was the isotopes – or you can say it was belief, willpower, determination.

Doesn't matter if it's a tumour or any other problem in life – you can sit there like a passenger and let it happen to you, or you can get up and do something about it. Fight your way out!

JOHN: Not out here.

RICK: Anywhere!

JOHN: That's nonsense. You don't fight against a wave. You rise and fall with it, or get swept right off the planet.

RICK: We need to get off our arses and do something!

JOHN: This isn't Outward Bound! You're not the great I-am talking to a bunch of wet-behind-the-ears schoolkids!

RICK, *enraged*: Yeah, well what about you, John? 'This boat will never capsize!' You're full of shit! Why should we listen to you?

JOHN: Please yourself. But I'm not diving today. And without me you'll be scratching to find anything.

He goes back to writing in his notebook. Boiling with frustration, RICK flings himself out. JIM and PHIL look at each other.

JIM: What about the LPG tanks, John? Couldn't we look for those?

JOHN: I've cut enough holes in this boat already. I'm not going to butcher it any further. (*He is aware this is not the most compelling argument.*) There's no telling how far the regulators have corroded. If those gas bottles exploded they'd tear this boat apart – and us with it.

> JIM *absorbs that. He follows* RICK *out and finds him sitting on the keel gazing out at the sea.* JIM *sits down beside him and also gazes out.*

RICK: What are we doing here?

JIM, *shrugging*: Maybe just so John can write about us in his book and make us all famous.

RICK, *scowling*: He's got no one and nothing to go back to. That's why he thinks bobbing around out here is so much fun. It's Heather and Mattie I care about. They're more important to me than anything!

JIM: Even being a playboy of the South Pacific?

> RICK *grins but then is wistful.*

RICK: You know I never told them, Heather and Mattie, how they're the only thing that really matters to me.

JIM: Come on, Rick. They know.

RICK: How are they supposed to know if I don't tell them? 'Specially as I didn't even know myself. (*He looks around.*) Why did it take flipping upside down on this shitheap to show me where I've stuffed it up?

JIM: For Christ's sake, Rick, I envy you. You've got a great life, the things you've achieved, everything you've done –

RICK: I always had to be number one at everything. Motorbikes, kayaks, photography . . . Who cares? (*He throws his arms open to the empty sea and sky.*) Who bloody cares! (*He slumps back.*) You know what? I don't even like photography.

JIM: I don't believe this. You're putting yourself down for being good at things?

RICK: I did them so people would like me. So they'd respect me. So they'd say, 'Here comes Rick Hellriegel.' But who was it they were liking? Who was it they respected? If I stopped doing whatever it was – if I stopped doing all of it – what would be left?

JIM *doesn't know what to say.*

It's taken this long to figure out, but I know *who* would be left. Heather. She's always liked me for who I am. No, more – (*he looks at* JIM) – she loves me. She knows every shitty thing about me. But she loves me. (*He turns and stares away, tears starting into his eyes.*) And I get this great realisation now, while I'm stuck out here floating to South America in a bathtub. And she probably thinks I'm dead.

JIM *puts his arm round* RICK'*s shoulder.*

JIM: We'll get out of here. We'll get back home and Heather'll say 'about time you showed up'.

RICK, *turning to look at* JIM: I never talked about any of this stuff before. I never *thought* about any of this stuff before. It's just – why now, when I can't use it?

JIM: You'll get to use it.

RICK *nods.*

RICK: Thanks, mate. (RICK *looks* JIM *in the eye intently.*) We need each other, Jim. That's the only way we're going to make it.

JIM *is powerfully affected. Their hands clasp, fingers gripping tight.*

JIM: Rick, I will always be here for you.

In the cave PHIL *swigs from a plastic bottle, then weighs it.*

PHIL: Water's getting low, John.

JOHN, *nodding*: Time to tap into the tanks.

> *He takes the bottle and climbs out into the flooded cabin.*
> *RICK and JIM come down as he squints up at a screw cap*
> *above him.*

JOHN: A hundred litres makes for a fair bit of pressure. Have to make sure I can get the cap back on after the bottle's filled.

> *He turns the cap gingerly like a safecracker, pauses as he*
> *feels it near the end of its thread, checks he has the bottle*
> *ready — then turns the cap and whips it off, pushing*
> *the mouth of the bottle up to the hole all in one quick*
> *motion. Rather than the gusher he expects, there is nothing.*
> *Not even a trickle.* JOHN *is stunned — then filled with a*
> *sickening suspicion.*

JOHN: Oh no.

> *Hearing this,* RICK, JIM *and* PHIL *glance at each other*
> *nervously.*

JIM: John?

PHIL: You OK, mate?

> JOHN *doesn't answer. He moves quickly across to a second*
> *tank on the other side. He spins the cap off without his*
> *previous hesitation, holds the bottle up — but to no avail.*
> *This tank also is empty. The others are now avoiding*
> *looking at each other, unwilling to legitimise what they*
> *can sense is bad news on the way.*

RICK: John?

> JOHN *hurries back into the cave and rolls over the top of*
> *the others.*

JIM: Hey!

PHIL: Careful!
RICK: What's going on, John?

> JOHN *unplugs one last small tank above their sleeping*
> *space. It like the others is dry.*

JOHN: There's no water in the tanks.
RICK: What!
JOHN: They must have drained through the vents.
PHIL: No water?
JIM: You're kidding me!

> *As* JOHN *goes into a largely redundant explanation of*
> *this catastrophe, the others stare into their separate thirst-*
> *maddened deaths by dehydration with eyes like saucers.*

JOHN: I designed the tanks with vents to let the air out as they
were filled. One way so nothing could get in. But when we
flipped, the water must have just poured out through them.
My, my. Fancy that. (*He looks round them.*) Oh dear.

JIM *laughs, breaking out of the scene.*

RICK: 'Oh dear'!
JIM, *laughing*: 'My, my'!
RICK: Just a few bottles between us and a lingering death by
thirst – and that's all he's got to say!
JIM: What about when – right in the middle of when things
were most miserable – he'd come out with –
JOHN: Well, aren't we having fun today?
RICK: Fun? Fun? (JIM *laughs.*) He was certifiable – a nutter!
JIM: I guess he just had a different way of looking at things.
RICK: A lunatic's way of looking at things!
JIM: He told me once he tried to be happy every day out there.
RICK: There you go!
JIM: No, it made sense, Rick.

JOHN *hunkers down with* JIM.

JOHN: It's not about preparation, Jim – what's on the outside. It always comes back to this. Am I prepared *here*? On the inside? Have I got what it takes to live? Not just to survive. But to live right here – as fully as I'd live anywhere else? Taking out of this everything there is to take. Everything I've been set here to learn.

JIM: You really believe that, John? That there's a point to all this?

JOHN: Sure. The question isn't: Why did we flip? Why has this happened to us? No, the real question is: Why aren't we dead? Why have we been given shelter, the means to live? Why is the cabin fractionally above the waterline? Why does it exactly fit the four of us and no more?

   You feel it, don't you, Jim? Something's meeting us halfway. Saying, 'Come on – show me what you've got – let's see what you're made of.'

JIM, *a little surprised*: Yeah . . . I guess I do feel that, John.

   RICK *has been watching them talk.*

RICK, *a little grudgingly*: When did he say all this?

JIM: Towards the end. Up on the hull one day. While you and Phil were being great white hunters and talking about motorbikes.

RICK: Better than some half-baked New Age crap.

JIM: Everybody's got their beliefs, Rick. Just because you don't share them –

RICK: While he was busy being so 'happy' – he wasn't doing a thing to get us out of there!

JIM: He was coping in his own way – just like Phil getting all depressed. (PHIL *lies immobile on the other side of* RICK, *staring up.*) At least John didn't just lie there day after day, hardly saying a word . . .

RICK: They were both dead weight!

JIM: What do you think John thought of us, Rick? If there was one thing that got in the way of him being happy – like he wanted to be – it wasn't the sea, or hunger, or even thirst, it was us. Always copping an attitude, trying to squash him down. And sometimes . . .

RICK: What?

JIM: Sometimes especially you.

Sound: Boat. The four of them are racked out in the cave. JOHN *reaches up with a felt pen to place a mark on the ceiling.*

JOHN: Well, well. (*No one takes the bait.*) If this calendar's right, – (*still no takers*) – it's my birthday today. (*He caps the pen.*)

PHIL: Happy birthday, mate.

JIM: Yeah, happy birthday, John.

There is a noticeable pause before RICK *begrudges –*

RICK: Happy birthday.

PHIL *sucks at his dry lips.*

PHIL: Must be time for our moisture by now, Jim.

JIM: Yeah, where's the vial?

They look around.

RICK: Come on. It was here when we had our ration this morning.

PHIL: We'll do without it – just estimate it.

RICK: No way. That's the measurement we agreed on.

PHIL: Well find the bloody thing before I die of thirst!

JOHN *finds it.*

JOHN: It's underneath you, Phillip.

He fills the vial, a three-ounce olive jar, with water so it's brimming to the top and gingerly, so as not to spill any, passes it down the line to PHIL.

Sound: Amplified hallucinatory fresh water sounds, and drinking sounds, as described through the following –

JIM: Thirst. I'd never felt anything like it before. Never would have believed that, all day every day, my mind could be completely occupied with thoughts of water: fresh water; water coolers; water bursting out of faucets; streams of it; lakes of it.

The refilled vial arrives at him. While JIM *drinks, the others studiously find something else to look at.* JIM *hands the vial back. It is refilled for* RICK *(squirt-round-the-mouth) then* JOHN *(down-the-hatch).*

JIM: We all had our particular style. There was the squirt-around-the-mouth-and-swallow, the make-it-last sip, or the down-the-hatch-in-one-go.

JOHN finishes, smacking his lips.

JOHN: Lovely.
JIM: Put the vial up where we'll find it next time.
JOHN, *hesitating*: I thought perhaps – we could have an extra tonight. So I can toast my birthday.

PHIL and RICK are quick with their usual responses.

PHIL: Good idea, mate.
RICK: I vote no.
JIM, *realising he's going to be left carrying the baby*: Great . . .

RICK and PHIL turn to him.

PHIL: Come on, Jim – look at what we've done today.

RICK: You know we can't afford it, Jim.

PHIL: We tied all that stuff on deck, re-did the bed, sorted the stores—

RICK: There's no sign of rain, we don't know how long we have to last, and that's another day's rations we'd be pouring down our throat.

> PHIL *and* RICK *watch on tenterhooks as* JIM *looks at* JOHN.

JIM: Sorry, John.

> *They lie back down:* RICK *a little sanctimonious,* PHIL *petulant,* JIM *guilty,* JOHN *hurt.*

> *Sound: Water sounds down to the amplified regular drip of fresh water into a deep clear well, like the stroke of a clock – torture to thirsty men . . .*

RICK, *breaking*: OK, so there were times I was a bit of a prick. But what about you with that cardboard chess-set?

> RICK *and* JIM *prop themselves on their elbows as* RICK *considers his move.*

JIM: Come on, Rick. My arm's going to sleep.

RICK: I'm thinking.

> JIM *moves uncomfortably, as does* RICK, *causing a ripple effect across* PHIL *and* JOHN.

JIM: Maybe we should have a time limit for moves.

RICK: Why? You got an appointment or something?

JIM: You take three times as long as me.

RICK: I should have all the time I want!

JIM: Why's it so important to you to win?

PHIL: It's just a game, mate.

RICK: It's a game *I'm* playing! Which has got nothing to do with you!

PHIL: It has when you take up too much bloody room while you're doing it.

He plumps down, which pushes RICK *so he inadvertently jolts the board, scattering some of the pieces.*

RICK: Phil, for Christ's sake!

JIM: This game is the only thing that takes my mind off dying of thirst! Or starving to death! And everything else to do with this whole shitty experience!

PHIL says nothing. JOHN pipes up.

JOHN: In that case we should all have a turn. I'll play the winner.

JIM: Fuck off, John. I don't want to play with you, I want to play with Rick!

PHIL sits up and scrambles out backwards, managing to poke, squash or otherwise inconvenience each of the others in the process, oblivious to their protests.

JOHN: Phillip!

RICK: Jesus!

Emerging onto the hull, PHIL sits on the keel moodily staring out.

Why does he do that *every* time? It's the most infuriating thing about him!

JIM: No way. The most infuriating thing is his volcanic belching.

RICK: Yeah, but worse than that is his toenails. How he's always curling them into you and scratching.

JOHN: For my money it's the way, every time there's a big wave, he throws himself up, whacks his head on the ceiling and dives for the hatch.

JIM: Demonstrating twenty times a day that if anything did

happen, he'd panic and we'd all drown.

RICK: And don't forget all the stuff he's lost through being careless.

JIM: Dragging it out with him when he backs out the hatch.

JOHN: My balaclava.

RICK: The knife.

JIM: Screwdriver.

JOHN: And that sheaf of garlic. (*This is a particularly sore point.*)

RICK: A whole sheaf of it.

JIM: Would have lasted months.

JOHN: The night we flipped he pulled all the drawers out upside down and lost everything.

RICK: Everything but his stupid lump of a sheepskin coat that's always getting in the way. (*Gives it a kick.*) Let's face it – he's a liability.

JIM: Come on, guys – he did try fishing yesterday.

Yesterday. PHIL *flourishes their one and only fishing rod.* JOHN *talks to him through the hatch.*

JOHN: You can't catch fish out here, Phillip.

PHIL: Thought I saw one in the hull a couple of days ago.

JOHN, *shaking his head*: Imagination.

PHIL: Gotta give it a burl, mate.

> *He disappears over the hump of the keel.*

RICK: Why can't you catch fish out here?

JOHN: No fish here.

RICK: This is the ocean. Where do you think you can catch fish – the Himalayas?

JOHN, *smiles a superior smile*: Waste of energy.

JIM: If it makes Phil feel better . . .

RICK: If it gets him out of my face.

They stop as there is a rattling, sliding sound on the skin of the hull on the side where PHIL *has clambered to fish.*

PHIL: Oops . . .

After a moment, PHIL *reappears over the hull, slides into the cave and lies still, staring at the ceiling. Pause.*

JIM: You didn't lose the fishing rod did you, Phil?
PHIL: Sure did, mate.

Pause.

RICK, *angrily*: No – what really got to me about Phil was the way he just lay there, hour after hour, not saying anything, not doing anything. Just waiting to die.

The scene has reverted to the bedroom. JIM *nods.*

JIM: That's pretty hard to lie beside. When you're doing everything you can not to wait to die.

JIM *glances at* RICK *a little awkwardly, but* RICK *plunges on.*

RICK: You don't just – let go like that! It's defeatist. It's self-pitying!

JIM *takes refuge in cheerfulness, arranging* RICK's *bedclothes.*

JIM: That reminds me, Rick – I read this article where this woman was dying too, but she recovered and—
RICK: Fuck you!
JIM: What? What did I say?
RICK: You said she was dying *too*!
JIM: I didn't mean it, Rick.

RICK: Yes you did! I'm not dying!

JIM: I know . . .

RICK: I'm going to beat this!

JIM: I know you are.

RICK: If you don't believe it you might as well piss off back to the States!

JIM, *out*: The emotional blackmail! The demands! It's a codependent's nightmare! Like when Rick gets diarrhoea – it's like we all get it.

RICK: Heather, I gotta go!

JIM: Our whole life revolves around it, around his needs.

RICK: Heather!

JIM: She's hanging out your washing, Rick. Let's try it just me and you.

> JIM *struggles to lift him and support him across the stage –*

RICK: Come on, come on. I'm crapping myself!

JIM: OK, Rick!

> *– to where he slumps down on the toilet.*

JIM, *out*: But brushing Rick's teeth, brushing his hair, confronting each new crisis or challenge his broken body throws forth –

RICK: Jim!

JIM: – I realise it's not a one-way street – (JIM *lifts him again for the return trip.*) – that I need him. Simply because he needs me. (*Back at the bed.*) Though there are times I wonder how much any of us can take.

RICK, *testy*: These pillows are too soft. Do you want me getting bedsores?

JIM: Rick drives us to make sure that everything is right, everything is as up to scratch as it can be. He sends his food back three or four times –

RICK: Too hot – too cold – too mushy – not mushy enough!

JIM: – until I want to scream. Until Heather does scream.

RICK: If you give up on me, I'm going to die!

> JIM, *sighs and turns front.*

JIM: Christmas Day.

Sound: Summer day, children –

JIM: Bright summer out on the lawn, boats gliding past on a light breeze up from the Sound, bringing the smell of cut flowers. I luxuriate in the dinner of turkey, glasses of wine, kids running round with their presents, lounging in the sun . . . the change from being tethered to Rick's side. Freedom for one light, bright, summer day. But he calls out.

RICK: Jim? Jim!

JIM: I don't want to go. (*Sound fades into the distance.*)

> His dim room smells stale and sick. He sits propped up, wasted to skin stretched tight over bone, a napkin under his chin smeared with food. I don't want to be here, I feel like I'm climbing back aboard the crippled *Rose-Noëlle.* I try to cut the conversation short, but he drags it out. Slowly I settle, sit down, grasp his frail hand, and my impatience slips away. I despise his wrecked body on which we endlessly drift. But if it's this bad for me, how much worse is it for him? It's a featureless sea. Nothing on the horizon. But I can crew a little more, drift a little further for my friend. For Rick.

Sound has gradually morphed into water lapping against the hull. JOHN stands on the keel and looks out, seeing something beautiful. With a mischievous grin he sticks his head down to the others.

JOHN, *fake plaintive*: Doesn't anybody want to come up on deck with me? (*The others stir, groaning, irritated at being disturbed.*) Doesn't anyone want to see this beautiful sunrise?

RICK: There's no such thing as a beautiful bloody sunrise out here.

JOHN withdraws back to the hull, still calling.

JOHN: I just thought you might like to come up –
RICK: Why doesn't he shut up?
JOHN: – and see this sailboat.
PHIL: Sailboat?

They look at each other for a split second before hurling themselves all together, struggling and scrambling to get out the exit and onto the hull. JOHN has a grin on his face as they erupt out to stand beside him and gaze out at the sight.

JOHN: She's a beauty, isn't she?
RICK: Quick, get the barbecue going!

RICK, JIM and PHIL spring into action, grabbing the barbecue which is tied into the centreboard slot on the hull, retrieving a bucket of woodchips, a rubber diving flipper and some crumpled, navigation charts, while PHIL dives below to get the matches. JOHN is slightly detached from this flurry, helping a little but gazing out at the white sails on the horizon with the quiet pleasure of a boat builder.

PHIL: Matches.
JIM: Come on. Let's get this thing lit!

The paper catches, but goes out. They try again –

RICK: Give me some shelter!

– and again.

JIM: It's not catching. The woodchips are too big!

PHIL: I've got some gas from the generator!

> *He splashes a cup of petrol over the contents of the barbecue.*
> RICK *flicks a match in and fire roars up, forcing them*
> *back.*

JIM: Wooo!
PHIL: That's more like it!

> RICK *drops the flipper on top, all but extinguishing the*
> *fire –*

PHIL/JIM: Uh-oh . . .

> *– before the flames emerge to lick round it, producing oily*
> *black smoke.*

RICK: Yes!
JIM: Just like on TV: Flipper Saves the Day!
PHIL, *looking up at the growing column*: They've gotta see that
  smoke!
RICK: What d'ya reckon – bacon and eggs for breakfast!
JIM: Followed by a lie-down in a bunk!
PHIL: A bunk each! No offence, but I never want to sleep with
  you bastards again!

> *They gaze out at the boat, willing it to turn, slow, show*
> *some sign that it has seen them.*

RICK: Come on!

> JIM *shades his hand to look up at the column of smoke,*
> *realising –*

JIM: The wind's catching the smoke . . .
PHIL: It's only a breeze!
JIM: It's spreading it out. (*He looks over at the distant sails again.*)
  From where they are it'd just look like a smudge.

RICK: If they see it at all.

JOHN says nothing. Clearly he has expected the attempt to be futile. Now, as dejection sets in, he offers –

JOHN: There shouldn't be a yacht out here.

RICK: *This* bloody yacht shouldn't be out here, that's for sure!

PHIL: What do you mean, John?

JOHN: I've never seen a boat like that out in the middle of nowhere.

JIM: So we're not nowhere?

JOHN, *looking at him*: Maybe not. (*He stretches, taking a last look at the sails.*) That's a good start to the day. What's for breakfast?

RICK, *indicating the barbecue*: Toasted flipper?

JIM, *out*: 'A good start'. Some day that turned out to be.

He joins the others in the 'cave', in the middle of a debate –

JOHN: It would take an hour for a ship to get by us anyway. I think once an hour is fine.

RICK: Bullshit. A ship would come and go in twenty minutes.

JOHN, *scoffing*: Not in my experience. I remember when we were in the Roaring Forties—

RICK: Hell with the Roaring Forties. That was twenty years ago. Ships were slower. We need to at least double the watch.

PHIL: Rick, we're having a hard enough time getting up on the hour for a look round.

RICK: You guys just don't want to get out of here. I'm telling you what to do and you don't even listen!

JIM: Let it go, Rick. It's not important.

RICK: It *is* important! We're talking about our lives here!

JOHN: Stop trying to be captain. I'm the captain here.

RICK, *incensed*: I'm not trying to be captain – and you lost all right to be the captain when we flipped! Nobody's captain!

We're all equal partners – and it's in everybody's interest to keep a better lookout and get out of here.

JIM: Relax, Rick. Let go of it.

RICK: John told us there weren't ships out here – but there *are*. We saw one! Don't you understand that?

JIM, *leaning into* RICK's *face*: Shut up. Just shut, the fuck, up!

> JIM *scrambles out onto the hull.*

PHIL: What say we go up and work on the generator, John?

JOHN: Sounds good to me, Phillip.

> *They leave* RICK *alone.*

JIM: As if that wasn't bad enough – then Rick really scared me . . .

> RICK *approaches* JIM *up on the hull.*

RICK: Jim, what don't you like about me?

JIM, *startled and taken aback, scrambling*: What? What do you mean? You're my friend – of course I like you.

RICK: No, I don't mean that. What is it people don't like about me sometimes?

JIM: Jesus, Rick, we're fighting just to survive here—

RICK: I need to know what my faults are. So I know what to do to become a better person.

JIM: Are you sure this is the right time for self-improvement?

RICK: I trust you to tell me, Jim.

JIM: Give me a minute will you, Rick?

> JIM *turns away from* RICK, *struggling with what to say, and addresses the audience.*

It's not enough to let me dehydrate to death in peace. Now I have to deliver an off-the-cuff critique of my best friend's character defects. I bet Columbus or Blackbeard the pirate never had to put up with this. (*He glances at* RICK.) But he

actually wants to know. He really wants my help. But what
if I tell him and he hates me? I'm depending on him – he's
all I've got onboard this tub. Worse, what if I tell him and
he says something back about me? But I can't say nothing.
He's relying on me. He's reaching out.

   (Jim *turns back to* Rick.) First off, Rick, this is really,
really hard to do. I mean, I like you. I really like you. I
think you're smart and brave and—

Rick, *impatiently*: Yeah, yeah, yeah – but what else?

Jim: Well, look, Rick, you've been a cop, an OB instructor, run
  your own business. You're used to being in charge.

Rick: So you're saying I'm high-handed, arrogant, a bully?

Jim: No! But—

Rick: What?

Jim: You remind me of John sometimes.

Rick: Of John?

Jim: You *do*. You think you're right and he thinks he's right. And
  you both think your way is the only way. (Rick *considers*
  this.) And you're real abusive to John sometimes, Rick. You
  know you are.

   Rick *nods.*

Rick: I'm going to try as hard as I can just to back off.

Jim: And . . .

Rick: Yeah?

Jim: Well – the way I've seen you treat Heather sometimes.

Rick: What do you mean?

Jim: Like when Mattie was born and you wouldn't rig up the
  laundry for a washing machine, so she had to scrub nappies
  by hand every day.

Rick: That's none of your – (*He catches himself, chews it over
  a moment, struggling with himself.*) You're right about
  Heather. I've been a real jerk. But it won't be like that when
  we get back. I swear.

JIM: You're not mad at me?
RICK: Course not. I really appreciate this.

>   JIM *sighs with relief, until* RICK *grabs his arm.*

>   Is there anything else you can think of?
JIM, *startled*: I'll let you know, alright!
RICK: Thanks, Jim.

>   *He retreats back to the cave.* JIM *watches him a moment.*

JIM, *out*: Sometimes, huddled into Rick for warmth – each day
    feeling his bones a little more clearly through the flesh, his
    thirst, hunger, pain the same as my own – I'd think, have
    I ever been as close to anyone as I am to him? And I'd
    wonder – even if we made it back – would I ever be as close
    to anyone again?
>   Maybe, in those first couple of months, Rick and I
    depended on each other a little too much. Perhaps if we'd
    looked outside of ourselves more, we'd have noticed there
    were four of us out there. And it was going to take all of us
    to survive.

>   JIM *joins* RICK *in the cave.*

RICK: He's drinking our water.
JIM: God, just the word – 'water'.
RICK: Eating our food.
JIM: *Losing* our food.
RICK: He's diminishing our chances of getting out of here.
    He's a Jonah. He's been nothing but deadweight since the
    beginning.
JIM: Let's make him walk the plank.

>   RICK *looks at him.*

Just kidding, Rick.

JOHN *squeezes into the cave.*

JOHN: He's coming down now.

PHIL *follows a moment later. The others shuffle round. There is an awkward pause.* PHIL *senses the atmosphere, sees everyone is looking at him.* JIM *breaks the silence.*

JIM: Phil, I think we all want to talk to you.

And they do. All at once. PHIL *looks from face to face as* JIM *picks on his habit of losing things and builds up to saying they care about him as a person,* RICK *gives an Outward Bound motivational speech on teamwork and the need to be able to rely on each other,* JOHN *waxes lyrical about the loss of the garlic and how they all want to get home. In the middle of this –*

PHIL: I fell off the boat. (*This is lost in the crosstalk until –*) I fell off the boat!

They stop.

Yesterday. I was squatting on the side trying to have a crap. A wave came up over the hull and washed me off. By the time I came back up and got my pants organised the boat was fifteen, twenty yards away. Just drifting off. (PHIL *looks round at them.*)

I tell you what, I thought floating around in an upturned trimaran was as bad as things could get. I've lain here staring at the ceiling for hours thinking about home, and comparing it to this ratshit hole. I'm sorry, John, but I've hated this bloody boat. Hated it.

But I soon changed my mind when I saw it drifting away from me. 'Cos you know what it looked like? All of a sudden it looked like home. It looked like a very desirable residence. Once you've had a close look at the rest of the neighbourhood. And, let me tell you, if I had an outboard motor strapped to me I couldn't have swum any faster.

The others are shocked – this has been a common nightmare for all of them.

RICK: Mate, you could have yelled out.
PHIL: It all happened so quick. I didn't get my breath back till I'd grabbed hold and pulled myself up again.
JIM: Why didn't you tell us?
PHIL: Figured you might just wish the wind had been blowing a bit harder.

The others glance at each other with a trace of guilt, but are sincere in their protestations.

JOHN/RICK/JIM: No, mate – not at all – no way.
JIM: We've got to stick together, Phil. I think that's what we've been trying to say to you.
PHIL, *nodding:*I've been thinking about it. Sure – I want to get off of here. But right now this is where I am. (PHIL *looks round at them and takes a breath.*) I *do* care. I want to get back to Karen and the kids. I'm going to try. I want to be back on the team.

It's an emotional moment. They welcome him back to the fold. So intent are they that they don't hear the ticking sound on the hull – until it builds up into a steadier rhythm.

JIM: It's raining.

They stare at each other a moment, listening.

It's raining!

They scramble wildly to put into action the prearranged plan, RICK *and* JIM *retrieving containers, –*

How many do we need?
RICK: Bring 'em all!

> – JOHN *and* PHIL *heading for the hull where* PHIL *spreads a plastic sheet and* JOHN *angles it down* –

JOHN: Come on, Phil. Like we practised –
PHIL: OK, John –

> – *channelling the run-off into a container held by* RICK.

RICK: That's good . . . That's good . . .

> *The rain intensifies into an exhilarating downpour, drumming in a cacophany on the hull and plastic sheet, drenching them.*

PHIL: Come on! Yes! Rain! Rain, you bugger!
JOHN: Don't lose a drop –
RICK: There's the first one!

> *The full container is passed to* JIM *and quickly replaced by an empty.* JIM *chugs on the water, almost dancing in exuberant delight.*

JIM: It works! It's water! Pure, fresh rainwater!
RICK: Woo-hoo!

> PHIL – *arms outspread holding the corners of the plastic sheet – lifts his face to the sky in 'Monsoon Girl' celebration.*

PHIL: Never underestimate the power of water!

> *As lights fade on the scene of joyous activity, the sound of the rain swoops up to obliterate everything. Music.*

Act Two

JIM *is brushing* RICK'*s teeth.*

JIM: Beautiful day outside. The Outward Bound bunnies have got the kayaks out. (*He crosses to the window to part the curtain.*) You might be able to see—

> RICK, *toothbrush left sticking out of his mouth, grunts.*

Too bright? Sorry.

> JIM *pulls the curtain to again, and goes back to retrieve the toothbrush. As he puts the brush and toothpaste away –*

You know what, Rick? I think I'm going to kind of miss your teeth. (*He starts brushing* RICK'*s hair.*) And your hair. I do a better job of it than my own.

RICK: Who's going to get me looking good for Heather?

JIM: I guess . . . Heather'll do it. Then act surprised and delighted. (*He imitates.*) 'Rick – you spunk!'

> RICK *grins lopsidedly.* JIM *puts the hairbrush away.*

Rick, what are you going to do with your half of the kayaking business?

> RICK'*s grin disappears. He shrugs.*

You're going to have to let go of it sometime.

RICK: I've got a few things on my mind besides kayaks.

JIM: You always said kayaking is where you're happiest. Sometimes when you're just lying here, times I've thought you're asleep but you're not, I figure that's where you are – out on the water, going for a paddle.

> *This is a bit too close for* RICK.

RICK: Why am I going to have to let go the business? Because I'm going to die?

JIM: That's not what I said.

RICK: I'm supposed to be dead already, aren't I? You were meant to be free to go off and write your book.

JIM: Rick, it's our last day.

RICK: Sorry for screwing up your schedule.

JIM: I'm ignoring you, Rick.

> *Pause. They ignore each other.* JIM *is first to break.*

You think I wanted you to get sick? That I want to leave you like this?

RICK: You're going – that means you want to.

JIM: And I suppose you wouldn't if you were me?

RICK: Hell no! I'd have gone months ago.

> JIM *can't help but laugh.* RICK *cracks a wry smile.*

You wouldn't catch me wiping your arse.

> JIM *pretends to smother him with a pillow.*

JIM: Hey, look what I've got. (*He takes out a packet of Full o' Fruit biscuits.*) Remember? (RICK *nods.* JIM *slides a line of the biscuits out of the packet, bends it and peels a biscuit off.*) Man, our entire day used to revolve around these. Hanging out for morning tea and our Full o' Fruit biscuit. Savouring it when it came. Craving the next one, a whole day away.

> *He offers it to* RICK, *who shakes his head.*

I could crumble it up for you?

> RICK *shakes his head again.* JIM *regards the biscuit almost with wonderment.*

Incredible. The way as soon as it rained and we had

enough water, it was like throwing a switch – and suddenly
everything was about food. Full-on daylong fantasies of
eating. Burgers, fries . . .

RICK: Roast dinner . . .

JIM: Cheesecake . . .

RICK: Ice-cream . . .

JOHN: Chocolate . . .

PHIL: Cream cakes . . .

They've segued back to the Rose-Noëlle.

JIM: No . . . No, what I want is the biggest burrito in the world
– stuffed with refried beans, ground pork, melted cheese
and chilli sauce dripping out of it . . .

JOHN: Burrito?

JIM: Tortilla bread wrapped round a filling.

JOHN: Oh, a tamale.

JIM: No, burrito.

JOHN: What you're describing is a tamale.

RICK: Jim's a Yank. He's from the States. I'd say he knows what
it's called.

JOHN: All I can say is when I was in San Diego in '69 they had
those and they were called tamales.

RICK: Can you believe this guy? He even knows better about
your own fantasies!

PHIL, *popping up*: Tea time, Jim?

JIM, *to distract from the tamale tension*: It's a bit early. But for
you, Phil – in honour of your special day . . .

PHIL, *rubbing his hands together*: Yes!

As JIM *organises the biscuits,* PHIL *squints out the hatch.*

RICK: No sign of Harry?

PHIL: Not yet. I told you I saw a fish. I was the first to see him.

JOHN: If it's the same one hanging round, could be a small shark
    – or a grouper.

JIM, *passing round*: One Full o' Fruit biscuit.

JOHN: Lovely.

> JIM *and* JOHN *lift their biscuits in salute to* PHIL.

JOHN/JIM: Happy birthday, mate!

> PHIL *acknowledges this and they eat enthusiastically, except
> for* RICK *who vacillates, staring at the Full o' Fruit biscuit
> in his hand.* JIM *notices, stares at him.*

JIM: I'll never forget watching you.

RICK: I'd promised myself I could do it. Give Phil my biscuit.
    For his birthday.

JIM: You hadn't told anyone. No one was expecting you to.

RICK: Such a lousy day. Cold and shitty outside. And cold and
    shitty inside. And I'm starving.

JIM: We all were.

RICK: Lost all the fat I could lose. My body was taking it from
    muscle now. Couldn't walk without my legs collapsing
    under me. My mind and my body pulled towards food like
    a magnet. (*He turns the biscuit.*)

    Sugar, crumbs, flour, fruit. I knew the taste of this
    biscuit. The smell. My body had smelt it now. It was like
    I'd already eaten it, digested it, burnt it. Factored it into my
    equations. And if I didn't eat it I'd be this much closer to
    death.

    But I'd promised myself.

JIM: We were dying of hunger for Christ's sake! That can't help
    but do things to you.

RICK: Told myself I was strong enough. To still act like a human
    being.

JIM: Normal human things – generosity, sharing – they just go.
    This is what we were becoming – animals who fight over

scraps. Like the day before, when Phil and I rolled over and saw that grain of rice someone had dropped.

JIM *and* PHIL *spy it at the same time and stab their fingers towards it, tussling and scrabbling to be first to capture the tiny miserable solitary grain.* PHIL *succeeds and pops it in his mouth.* JIM *watches ruefully.*

JIM: Good?

> PHIL *works the grain round his mouth and delivers it back into his hand on the tip of his tongue.*

PHIL: It's just a little bit of wet paper. Rolled up. (*He shows* JIM *and then flicks it back into his mouth.*) Not bad though.

RICK: Look at Phil. He's more of a bottomless pit than any of us. He wouldn't appreciate it.

JIM, *nodding*: He'd just wolf it straight down and look round for more.

> RICK *lifts the biscuit to his mouth and nibbles along its edge. He stops himself with an effort. He steels himself – holds the biscuit out to* PHIL.

RICK: Happy Birthday, Phil.

> PHIL *stops dead, stares at* RICK, *down at the biscuit, up at* RICK *again. Pause.* JOHN *and* JIM *are staring too.*

PHIL: Thanks.

> *He takes the biscuit. It disappears into his mouth in a single chomp.* RICK *relaxes, satisfied. He hasn't let himself down. He's made a point.*

Sound: Boat sounds fade back under bedroom for a few lines –

RICK *picks up the packet of biscuits with his good hand.*

RICK: They don't have these in the States. You'd better take
some home with you.

JIM, *looking at his half-eaten biscuit*: You know what I think?
They're just not making them like they used to.

PHIL, *suddenly spotting*: Harry's back!

Back on the Rose-Noëlle. *Everyone springs into action in a tangle
of limbs,* JOHN *clearing the way for* JIM *to grab the landing net, while*
PHIL *crowds to the hatchway trying to see.*

JIM: Where is he?

PHIL: He was over by the dinette – must have poked into a
locker.

JIM: Out of the way, Phil!

> RICK *grabs* JIM's *ankles as he leans out with the makeshift
> net.*

I can't see him.

RICK: Take it easy. He'll be back.

> *They hold their breath.*

JIM: There he is!

> *As* JIM *watches like a hawk, slowly dipping the net,* PHIL
> *and* RICK *barrack simultaneously –*

PHIL: Go for your life, mate. That's dinner. Come on, Jim.

RICK: Take your time. Think about what you're doing, Jim.
Keep your eye on him.

PHIL: Crikey dick he's a big bugger!

JIM: Rick, hold my legs! (*He scoops, and lifts the sudden weight of Harry clear of the water.*) I've got him! Jesus, I've got him!
PHIL: He's got 'im, John – he's got 'im!
RICK: Shit hot!
PHIL: Hold onto him, Jim lad!

> *Holding the net up,* JIM *half-wriggles is half-dragged by the others back into the 'cave'.*

JOHN: It *is* a grouper.
RICK: A *big* grouper! Can't catch fish in the ocean eh, John?
PHIL, *as Harry erupts in thrashing*: Look out!
JIM: Get him!

> *They all throw themselves at Harry, pummelling and whacking with anything that comes to hand, in a largely ineffectual chaos of slippery fish, confined space and confusion.* PHIL *rears back –*

PHIL: Outta the way!

> *– and throws his full weight across Harry in a grand slam.* PHIL *comes up with the grouper clutched to his chest like a lover.*

Calm down, Harry. You're going to be well taken care of now. (*Ardent.*) Oh, this is a big fish, John. A big fish.

> JOHN *takes his knife and slits Harry down the belly.* RICK *and* PHIL *react with disgust as the guts fall out, but* JOHN *and* JIM *take more interest.* JIM *holds up two small fish.*

JIM: Look what's inside him – a couple of half-digested herring.
JOHN: They'll be good. Save them.
RICK: *Save* them?
PHIL: I'll pass on that, mate.
JOHN, *scooping out one of Harry's eyes with his knife*: Oh my, there's a lot of fluid in these eyes. Want one, Jim?

He flips it to Jim, *who holds it up as if he's going to pop it in his mouth.*

Jim: Mmm, succulent.

Rick, *grossed out*: You *eat* that?

Phil: If you jokers are going to eat guts – it's only fair Rick and I get a bit extra of the flesh.

Jim: Hey, come on, Phil. We're happy to share. (*He shoves the eye at a queasy looking* Phil.) Our guts are your guts.

John: Sashimi, Jim?

Jim: My thoughts exactly, John.

As John *slices,* Jim *prepares, and the other two drool.*

Thin slices of raw fish, a little lemon juice and ground pepper from our salvaged spice rack. Allow to marinate for – ten seconds . . . And, chow down!

They all sit back with a collective sigh, replete, rubbing their stomachs.

Rest in peace, Harry.

Rick: Goodbye, Harry, we hardly knew you.

Phil *belches.*

John: There'll always be fish here now. (*The others look at him.*) With all the barnacles growing on the hull we've become a floating reef. That attracts the fish. They'll always be here now. (*This is said with the same unassailable certainty as when he pronounced they'd never catch fish.* Rick *shakes his head.*)

Jim, *out*: Soon we're fishing every day. Not for grouper like Harry, but for the kingfish that swarm in the pool between the main hull and one of the outriggers.

As they move to their 'fishing' positions, Jim *confers with* Rick.

You just have to accept it, Rick. Phil's best with the gaff.
He's quick and he's accurate and he gets fish where the rest
of us can't.

RICK, *making some adjustments to the landing net*: I accept it. I
just still can't understand it. I mean – Phil . . .

JIM: Look at him. He's so in love with food that he'll pour
the kind of concentration into stalking a fish that's been
noticeably lacking in any of his other attempts to help.

> PHIL *suddenly lunges with the gaff, and triumphantly lifts
> a fish.*

PHIL: You beauty!

JIM: Hey, Phil the Hook! The Great White Hunter!

> *But the kingfish twists off the gaff and plops back in the
> water.*

PHIL: Bugger!

RICK, *crossing*: Right. Getting them on the gaff is one thing,
keeping them on's another. That's why you've got to wait
for me to back you up with the net, Phil. We gotta work in
together, get synchronised.

PHIL: Yeah, well enough chit-chat, mate – get in behind.

JIM: Hours go by – Phil waiting, watching, gaff trailing in
the water, and with Rick like his shadow behind with the
landing net.

> PHIL *gaffs another kingfish,* RICK *scoops the net under it
> and lifts it clear of the water.*

RICK: Nicely done, mate – bang on the right spot.

PHIL: You were right there with the net too, mate. (PHIL *takes
the fish out of the net and holds it up.*) Lovely kingfish. But I
reckon yesterday's was better. (*He hands it up to* JOHN.) All
yours, John.

JOHN *guts and fillets it with impressive facility, watched by* JIM.

JIM: No doubt about it, John – you're a maestro.

JOHN: Used to do this for a living at one time.

JIM, *transferring the offal to jars*: Head . . . guts . . . and the precious fillets.

JOHN, *holding one up*: Lovely bit of fish. Beautiful grain, just the right colour . . .

JIM: Imagine how that would fry up . . . golden, inside pure white flaking apart, melting in your mouth.

> JOHN *salivates.*

I'd kill for some hot food! John, are you *sure* we can't find those gas bottles and rig something up?

> JOHN *looks from the fillet to* JIM *and back again. He is tempted, very tempted.*

JIM, *out*: And that's why, that very same night – right in the cave –

> PHIL *collapses back, satiated, from the little homemade gas cooker they're grouped around.*

PHIL: God, that was good.

RICK: You couldn't get better than that in any restaurant.

PHIL: Look at us. All mod cons. We've got light, warmth –

RICK: This place is finally going to dry out!

PHIL: – hot food in our belly.

JIM, *out*: Our life on the *Rose-Noëlle* neatly divides into two phases – Before Gas and After Gas. It was the coming of civilisation. We'd been living in the Stone Age – and now we knew it. And it was all thanks to— *[me]*

JOHN, *smug*: Glennie ingenuity – a little know-how. I keep telling you blokes, anything's possible if you just look at it the right way.

JIM, *out*: I don't believe it! For weeks I ask, suggest, cajole – then when he finally decides to try something, and it works out, he acts like he's King Kong and it's all his idea. (*He stops and thinks.*) Is this what it's like to be a woman?

JOHN, *writing in his notebook*: Now, what were those spices you used, Jim?

JIM: Oh, a little bit of this, little bit of that.

PHIL: Great chefs never give up their secrets, eh Jim?

RICK: How about we all take turns cooking?

> *This comes out of left field. The others are surprised.* JIM's *silence is eloquent.*

JOHN: I think Jim's been coming up with some lovely meals. I'm perfectly happy with him being the cook.

PHIL: Been doing a bloody good job, Jim. Don't know how to cook anyway.

JIM, *glancing at* RICK: Case closed.

> RICK *shrugs and heads for the hull where he hunkers down over something he's working on.* PHIL *then* JIM *follow.*

Later on, I come out and find Rick working on the new landing net that we'd both designed and were going to make together. He doesn't acknowledge it, doesn't even look at me . . . But it's a slap in the face – and meant to be.

Another day he asks me –

RICK: What say I help you cook dinner?

JIM, *glancing at him*: Sure, Rick. (*He heads into the cave to join* JOHN.) But I don't tell him when I start. (*Cooking, he holds a spoon up for* JOHN *to taste.*)

JOHN: Mmm. That's a lovely broth, Jim.

> RICK *has arrived in the entrance to the cave in time to witness this.* JIM *looks guilty in the face of* RICK's *accusing*

stare. RICK *turns back angrily, to rejoin* PHIL *on the hull.* RICK, *weak, struggles to clamber up the hull.* PHIL *comes to his aid.*

PHIL: Having a bit of trouble there, mate?

RICK: This hull seems to get higher every day.

PHIL: Tell ya what I'll do. I'll dive into the outrigger, pull that ladder out. If I lash it up here we can use it for stairs.

RICK: Thanks, mate.

JIM: Suddenly Rick and I are not really talking anymore. Not like we used to.

RICK *and* PHIL *head back into the cave and flop down beside* JOHN *and* JIM, *the others more exhausted and immobile than* PHIL

PHIL: What do ya reckon you'll do with this boat when she floats ashore, John?

JOHN, *shrugging*: Have to sell her, I guess.

PHIL, *considering*: She's a tidy little boat.

RICK: When it's right way up.

PHIL: I'll buy her off you. What are you asking?

JOHN, *smacking his lips*: Suppose I could let her go for ten thousand.

PHIL: Bit steep, mate. Now, eight thousand . . .

JOHN, *sighing, finding this turn of conversation a little depressing*: I'll think about it.

One thing's for sure, the *Rose-Noëlle*'d do you a lot better than that concrete monstrosity you've got back in Picton.

PHIL: Wait a minute, John. That's a bloody nice boat.

JOHN: It'll sink like a stone as soon as a whale hits it.

PHIL: That's my home you're talking about, John. That's where Karen and the kids live.

JOHN: Well at least you have something to go back to, Phillip. You don't know how lucky you've got it.

RICK: Hey, Phil, it's Friday night. Pub night.

PHIL, *going off into a reverie*: Yeah. I could just go a pint about now. And a cigarette. Haven't had one in years.

JOHN: Less time in the pub and you would have had that boat of yours seaworthy years ago.

RICK: Nobody asked you, John. What are you always picking on Phil for, anyway?

PHIL: No worries, mate. I can hold my own with John. Whose turn on watch? (*No answer.* PHIL *looks round his torpid crew mates.*) Crikey dick, do I have to do all the work round here?

As PHIL *goes up for a look round,* JIM *comes forward.*

JIM: Maybe it's not true, but I feel like Rick talks about me to Phil. Maybe he tells Phil all the things he doesn't like about me. John confides in me that he's never liked Rick – and now he doesn't like Phil either. I don't want to hear it.

I miss Rick. I miss having him to bounce ideas off, miss his support, and being able to give my support to him. I miss our talks, when it was just me and him and we were really talking.

I want to confront him about it, straighten everything out. But there's too many broken parts to know where to begin. Anyway, I tell myself, he started it – it's up to him to make the first move.

It's as uncomfortable and as painful as the breakup of any relationship I've had with a woman. And here we can't get away from each other. There's no place to run, no place to hide. The one thing I thought I could rely on on this boat is now also adrift.

JIM *finds* RICK *squatting – pants down – on the side of the boat, grimacing.*

JIM: Thought a wave might have washed you off.
RICK: Still here, mate.
JIM: Any luck?

> RICK *shakes his head, stands up shakily, pulling his pants up. He buckles and falls down on one knee.* JIM *helps* RICK *up.*

You OK?
RICK: Just got a bit of a tummy ache.
JIM: So would I if I'd only shit twice in three months.
RICK: Thought drinking that cup of vegetable oil might have helped.
JIM: I'm worried about you, Rick. You're weak, your eyes are sunken, you're falling over all the time. Even your speech is starting to slur.
RICK: Next you'll be telling me I'm full of shit.
JIM: I think it's time you faced up to something, Rick.
RICK: What?
JIM: The battery tester. (*He produces it, like a large plastic syringe, or turkey baster, full of vegetable oil.*) Except 'facing up' is probably not the appropriate term.

> RICK *stares at the battery tester dubiously.* PHIL *and* JOHN *don't know where to look.*

Ah, lie on your side, I guess.

> RICK *does so slowly, the others moving to accomodate.*

RICK: Thanks for doing this for me, Jim.
JIM: What are boat buddies for? (*There is an awkward pause.*) OK. Ready for this? (RICK *flicks him a sarcastic glance.*) Sorry, stupid question. (JIM *steels himself.*) Right. Pull your pants down.

Rick, *moving to, but hesitating*: Maybe I'll give it one more try.

> *He quickly wriggles out.* Jim, John *and* Phil *look at each other.* Jim *brandishes the home-made enema.*

Jim: Anyone else while I'm waiting?

> (*Out.*) You wouldn't believe it, but when Rick came back in –

> Rick *re-enters, a big smile on his face.*

(*Surprised.*) Success?

Rick, *nodding, grasping* Jim's *arm for emphasis*: And what success!

Jim, *looking at the unused battery tester*: That's what I call effective.

Sound reverts to bedroom –

As Jim *helps* Rick *climb back into bed –*

Jim: Seems like your bowels have been a major part of my life.

Rick: One less thing you have to worry about after today.

Jim: Rick . . .

Rick: You think I like it? Needing you or Heather to help me shit? Being changed like a baby?

Jim: Nobody's complaining.

Rick: I am.

Jim, *not knowing what to say*: That's not like you, Rick. You're the one who says we make our own luck.

Rick: Why has this happened to me? Again?

Jim: I don't know.

Rick: I thought I was the strongest on that boat. But you, Phil – even bloody John Glennie – you're running around out there, getting on with your lives. Why not me? Why am I the one kept back in school? Is it my fault?

JIM: Come on, Rick.

RICK: Is it some kind of weakness in me that's caused this?

JIM: You can't blame yourself. That doesn't make sense.

RICK: I was so busy 'being a man'. Stand tall. Stand fast. Don't
bend in case you break. It's like this tough shell I put on just
got harder and harder – protecting what was soft inside. But
trapping it too. (*He bites his lip.*) I can't tell Heather, Jim.

JIM: Tell Heather what?

RICK: I can't tell her – I'm really, really tired. Tired of trying.
Just sick of all this.

> JIM *grips* RICK's *hand.*

I used to want so much. Running to grab hold of everything
I could. Now all I want is to be near my wife and my son,
to get out of this bed, walk through the house and down to
the beach to take them kayaking. I want to be able to show
Mattie how to hold the paddle, get his movement smooth
and strong. For Heather and I to take him exploring the
Sounds. To show him places. To show him me. But that
can't happen, can it Jim?

JIM: Rick, I would love that as much as you.

RICK: Mattie's way too small. It'll have to wait till he grows.
I've just got to grow stronger too. (*He shakes his head.*) But
I've tried everything I know how. What am I supposed to
do that I haven't already been doing? What would John
Glennie do if it was him in this bed – pretend he was
having fun?

JIM: Maybe.

RICK: How?

JIM: Do you remember your birthday? On the *Rose-Noëlle*?

JOHN: Phillip . . .

PHIL *glances up as* JOHN *points out something in the sky.*

RICK: Birthday . . . ?
PHIL: Jim! Rick!

> PHIL *traces something gliding through the sky and down to*
> *the water nearby. The four form up on the hull, intently*
> *following its flightpath. A plane? No –*

JIM: The albatross. Majestic skimmer of the mid-ocean swell.
JOHN: Bird of good omen.
RICK: Wandering solo navigator at one with the elements.
PHIL: Lunch.
JOHN, *hoisting a rope threaded with*: Pick your fish head, Jim
lad.
JIM, *choosing with the air of a gourmet*: Just the right tang of
putrescence while still retaining enough firmness to anchor
the hook. (*He hooks the fish head on a length of fishing line,*
whirls it round his head and throws.)
PHIL: Good throw, Jim! (PHIL *adopts the role of the albatross,*
an extension of his normal rapacious, panic-prone, slightly
goony self. He cocks his head greedily at the bait.) He sees it. I
know what that is, he says. Rotten fish head – my favourite
flavour.

> PHIL *sidles round the bait, head cocked, then with a rush*
> *grabs it and tries to do a runner with it, feet furiously*
> *paddling across the top of the water in the albatross's*
> *ungainly lift-off routine.*

JIM: He's got it! He's got it!
JOHN: Hold on!

> *Doinngg! The line comes up taut, whipping the fish head*
> *out of* PHIL's *mouth.* PHIL *nosedives and crashes into the*
> *water.*

JIM: Lost him.

> PHIL *comes up squawking indignantly. He composes his albatross self, and eyes the miscreant fish head.*

PHIL: Like to play hard to get, eh?

> PHIL *paddles back to the fish head, acting nonchalant and uninterested, perhaps whistling. He makes a sudden dart at the fish head, grabs it, points his head straight to the sky, opens his throat and in several staccato gulps swallows the fish head.*

Ha-ha! Got you!

JIM: Got him!

PHIL, *checking his watch*: Good lord, look at the time. (*He paddles off busily.*)

JOHN: Ready . . . Pull!

> *As* PHIL/*albatross reaches the end of the slack,* JIM *heaves on the line.* PHIL *is abruptly pulled round with a startled squawk.*

Keep the tension on! Play him!

> PHIL *plants his feet and back-pedals furiously with his wings. He retches, trying to regurgitate the firmly lodged fish head.*

PHIL: If you feel that strongly about it, have your fish head back. No, really, I insist.

JIM, *steadily dragging in the thrashing albatross*: God, he's big! What do I do with him now?

JOHN: Leave him to me.

> *He grabs* PHIL/*albatross and tries to wring his neck.* PHIL/*albatross squawks and struggles powerfully.*

Pass me the knife.

> JIM *passes over a diver's knife.* JOHN *saws at the albatross's throat with it. As blood runs out over the deck the albatross's struggles subside. Moment of silence.*

JIM: Crimson splashes of blood on the keel.
JOHN: Baptising the pristine yellow.
RICK: You know what killing an albatross means.

> *They all nod solemnly, before –*

ALL: Ancient Mariner Barbecued Burritos! (JOHN *says* 'tamales'.)

> *Yes! They spring into action, each working on the albatross, the barbecue, the frying pans, or the ingredients.*

JOHN: Skin, debone, and cube one medium albatross.
PHIL: Marinate in vinegar and brown sugar.
RICK: Chuck another flipper on the barbie. Heat two frypans.
JIM: Roll out flour-and-water dough into tortillas. Fill with a tablespoon of baked beans.
RICK: Sauté seabird cubes for four minutes and combine with gravy mix until it thickens.
JOHN: Arrange Emperor of the Southern Seas on a little rice.
RICK: Whip up a Mexican bean sauce out of what's left in the can, some garlic water, one extralong little fingernail's worth of cumin and chilli.
PHIL: Salivate freely throughout.
JIM: Then pour the sauce over precisely equal portions of burritos.
JOHN: Tamales.

> *As* RICK *opens his mouth to take issue,* JIM *cuts him off.*

JIM, *to* RICK: Just don't buy into it, Rick. – And place beside steaming albatross chunks.

*Each looks at his plate of the finished product for a moment,
hardly able to believe it. As they move to eat –*

Maybe – (*They stop.*) – since this is such a special day for us,
we should each give our own thanks.

*They close their eyes and silently say their own version of
grace.* PHIL *finishes, his lips moving rapidly. He opens his
eyes and, not able to wait for the others, digs in.* RICK *is
next, then* JOHN. PHIL *starts to moan in ecstasy, causing*
JIM *to open his eyes and start. Soon they are all moaning.*

RICK: The flavours . . . The flavours!
JOHN: Oooaah. L-o-v-e-l-y!

This turns into a chant of –

JIM: Tangy.
RICK: Spicy.
JOHN: Red.
PHIL: Rich.
JIM: Thick.
RICK: Sweet.
JOHN: Beefy.
PHIL: Warm.

As they finish, PHIL *emits a gargantuan belch and speaks
for them all.*

Not bad, mate.
JIM: Thanks, Phil.
PHIL: I was speaking to the albatross.

Pause – filled with deep and abiding satisfaction.

JIM: Cup of tea?
PHIL: Stay there, Jim. I'll get it.
RICK: I'll put the water on before the barbie burns out.

PHIL *goes down into the hull. When he returns he is carrying 'The Bear' – the sheepskin coat, painstakingly dried out from the soaking frigid lump it was. Passing* RICK, PHIL *drapes the coat over his shoulders.*

PHIL: Happy birthday, mate. (RICK *looks incredulous.*) Fluffed up as good as new once she'd dried out.

RICK: I can't take this, Phil. Your brother-in-law gave it to you. It's family.

PHIL: Hey, ya look just the job in it. (*He rubs his stomach.*) Won't fit me for long when I get back.

RICK, *touched*: Thanks, Phil. (*He slips his arms into the sleeves and admires himself in it.*) Shit hot!

JIM: 'Happy birthday to you . . .'

JOHN *and* PHIL *join in singing 'Happy Birthday'. Tears spring into* RICK's *eyes.*

RICK: Jesus . . .

The singing halts.

JIM: Rick?

RICK *struggles with his emotions.*

RICK: I didn't want to look at the sunrise. I didn't want even one moment of being happy out here. Just wanted to stay focused on getting out – getting home. (*He looks at them.*) But this has been one of the best birthdays of my life. The truth is I couldn't have enjoyed it more if I'd been anywhere else.

It doesn't make sense. To be content. Here.

Pause.

JOHN, *tongue in cheek*: Well, I remember on *my* birthday – you guys wouldn't even let me have an extra vial of fizz-pop.

True enough. RICK *considers his churlishness.*

RICK: OK, John, you just pick a day and we'll have a special birthday treat for you.
PHIL: Yeah! How about a dessert?
JIM: John's just dessert.
JOHN: Sounds good to me.
PHIL: Should we have it now, John?

The others laugh.

JOHN: We've had quite enough today. We'll have it when *I* want to have it.
PHIL: Righto, John.

Sound reverts to bedroom –

RICK, *tired and weak, props himself against his pillows.*

RICK: Did we ever get that dessert in the end?
JIM: Sure. The night before we landed.
RICK, *remembering*: Before the fight – over the strobe.

JIM *nods.*

Dessert. He couldn't wait to desert us. Jumping out of the helicopter on Great Barrier the moment he caught sight of that journo he'd been hanging out to talk to.
JIM: He wasn't just some two-bit newspaperman, Rick – he was John's friend.
RICK: Couldn't wait to act the big man for the media, get on the lecture circuit, write his book. Captain Courageous.

JIM *says nothing, feeling the parallel a little too acutely.*

We were a team! For better or worse. But he bailed on us at the first opportunity!

JIM: Rick . . . !

RICK: What?

JIM: You tried to get the helicopter pilot to drop you off at your parents' place.

> RICK, *effectively pulled up, half-grins.* JIM *sits beside him.*

It did feel weird – after four months John suddenly not there. Must be weirder for you, that's the last you saw of him.

RICK: I'm coping.

JIM: You didn't get to say goodbye.

RICK: Not much good at sentimental farewells. (*He lies back, exhausted.*)

JIM: You know, as we took off, I looked down and I could see John running across the lawn to his friend and hugging the life out of that guy. Just – so delighted to see him.

RICK, *sleepy*: Yeah . . . What's your point, mate?

JIM: It made me realise how lonely John had felt all the time we were adrift – without anyone he really thought of as his friend. And it made me glad – that I had my friend with me the whole time.

> RICK *has drifted off into a doze.* JIM *looks at him, breaks away to speak to the audience.*

Sometimes I look at Rick and I think he's still got more in his life than I've managed to live in mine. When Heather comes in here with a hiss and a roar, shoves in beside him, slings his arm round her, and Rick lights up with that lopsided grin of his, I'm envious of a dying man. Even of how they fight – the way they never let each other get away with anything. They still care enough to get pissed off.

   It makes me realise I've never had that. Never had a woman who would grapple with me all the way down to death. Who would want me that powerfully. And me want her – as strongly and wildly as Rick wants Heather right now. Wants his wife. Not for what she does for him, or for the space she fills, but for the way he feels alive with her. The way she treats him as alive – when no one else ever leaves this room without a goodbye face. When people look at his frozen arm and useless leg as dead, at him as half-dead, crawling with death.

And what does Heather say to him? Shove over, can't you? Don't take up the whole bloody bed.

I want that. Want someone I can jump in beside, even on her deathbed, to be warmed by her as much as I give her my warmth. I want, as I die, for the last thing I feel to be the woman I love shaking me, saying: 'Shove over – give me my half. Deal with me. Play with me.'

But where do I go to start to find that for myself? Here – where there's nothing on the horizon? Where I strain my eyes day after day but can't see where we're heading.

This voyage with Rick has lasted twice as long as the one we took together on the *Rose-Noëlle*. And still there's no end. The end I've watched and waited for. And wanted. Not just for me but for Heather and Rick himself – while all the time assuring him that I don't believe it will ever come. I've tried to fulfill the pact I made on the keel of the *Rose-Noëlle*: that I would always be here for him. I've wanted to stay here, to be with him when he dies. But he hasn't died. I'm no longer sure he even will die. He's fought and fought and fought against it. Until that fight has exhausted us all.

It's not me who's dying. But my horizons, like Rick's, have shrunk to the size of this room. As claustrophobic as the cave on the *Rose-Noëlle*. I can't drift any more. I need to sight land again. My land. My life.

RICK, *mumbling in his sleep*: Bluebottles . . .

JIM: What's that, Rick?

Sound: Sea lapping against the hull –

RICK *wakes, and points down into the water around the hull.*

RICK: Bluebottle jellyfish – look. Phil and I know for a fact they only occur off the coast of New Zealand.

JIM: Phil reckons he won't believe we're near land till he sees a gannet.

> *Sound: Gannet noise.*

PHIL, *popping his head up*: Bloody hell! (*He pops back in.*)

JIM, *out*: But every time we think we see something – it turns out to be another cloud. I've got careful of disappointing myself – or anyone else.

> JIM *sits on the hull beside* RICK. JIM *lifts his arm and points.* RICK *squints, then registers something. He furrows his brow, looks away, and back again. He glances at* JIM, *who meets his eye for a long moment.* RICK *shrugs.* JIM *turns away.* RICK *catches* JOHN'*s eye and points.* JOHN *gazes out at the horizon. Each nurses their own hope, not able to bear to see it in the others' eyes.* PHIL *mooches round, stretches . . .*

JOHN: What do you think, Phillip?

PHIL: Eh?

> JOHN *gestures out.* PHIL *takes one look and erupts in glee.*

Oh yeah, shit, that's land! (*He dashes to a vantage point, shading his eyes, doing a sailor's hornpipe of delight.*) Fan-bloody-tastic, that's land! Yeah, that's land, John! It's land alright!

> *They all stare in painful hope.*

JIM, *fervent*: Just let it be there tomorrow morning. (*He closes his eyes then opens them again.*) And it is. The fuzzy blob a little clearer, more distinct. A little closer.

JOHN: By my guess we're about thirty miles out.

RICK: It's the Hauraki Gulf – it's gotta be.

JIM: Auckland. Downtown. We're going to tie up at the docks and walk up Queen Street to McDonald's!

RICK: Could slip past. But we're more likely to hit Great Barrier Island.

They stand staring.

JOHN: You know, I think we have the record now.

They look at him, uncomprehending.

PHIL: Eh?

JIM: What are you talking about, John?

This is something he has never mentioned before.

JOHN: The Guinness Book. A hundred and eighteen days – it's the record. You blokes are going to be famous.

RICK: Who gives a fuck, John?

JIM: John, I really don't give a shit about any record. I just want to get on with my life.

PHIL: All I want is to get back to Karen and the kids.

They leave JOHN *and go below, shaking their heads.*

JIM: We couldn't sleep that night. John went up on the hull for a while.

JOHN *climbs into the cave and lies down.*

JOHN: Just think – a couple of months ago we would have been excited to see a boat.

RICK: What are you talking about?

JOHN: There's another ship out there.

PHIL: What! (*He sits up suddenly, banging his head.*)

JOHN: It's too far away to signal.

> PHIL *crawls out, has a look, excitedly clambers back in,*
> *landing on top of them again.*

PHIL: John, John, where's that strobe? I'm going to signal her!

> PHIL *is scrambling over him, opening and scrabbling out*
> *the contents of a locker.* JOHN *tries to block him.*

JOHN: No you're not.

PHIL: Shit, John, that boat's really close!

JOHN: You can't even see its navigation lights! You'd just waste
your time and the battery!

RICK, *weighing in on Phil's side*: Yeah, and you can't catch fish
in the ocean!

> *They scrabble,* JOHN *struggles with them.*

JOHN: Leave that strobe alone!

PHIL: The hell I will! Get out of the way!

RICK: Yeah, John, shift your carcass!

JOHN, *grabbing the strobe from* PHIL: Who do you think you are?
This is my strobe! These are my things! My boat! You've
been helping yourself to the whole bang lot for four months!
You've got no business taking anything! I'm in command
here! You do what I say!

PHIL: Bloody hell with you, John! You need your head read!

> *They grapple until* PHIL *and* RICK *succeed in wresting the*
> *strobe away from* JOHN. *They turn and scuttle out with*
> *it.*

RICK: Come on, Phil. That ship's getting away!

> JOHN *is seething volcanically, rocking back and forth in*
> *paroxysms of rage.* JIM *watches him nervously.*

JIM: John?

> *Suddenly* JOHN *slams down his fist and bursts out of the cave.*

John!

> JIM *makes to follow him but* JOHN *has stopped short, staring at the sight that confronts him.* RICK *is swaying on a staggering* PHIL's *shoulders, holding on with one hand, waving the strobe with the other.* JOHN *gazes at this, then withdraws into the cave, his body wracked with strange spasms.* JIM *looks at him anxiously.*

What's the matter, John? Are you alright?

> JOHN's *chokes and spasms turn out to be laughter which now erupts. Tears stream out of his eyes as he rolls back and forth.*

JOHN: If you want . . . If you want to see something funny . . .

> *It's all he can do to gesture in the direction of the hull. Puzzled,* JIM *crawls out and takes in the sight of* RICK *and* PHIL. *He doesn't share* JOHN's *reaction. He crawls back into the cave where* JOHN *is only now recovering.*

Isn't that the funniest thing you've ever seen!
JIM, *whining*: John, it isn't funny to me.

> JOHN *continues to chuckle as* PHIL *and* RICK *return.*

RICK: That ship had to be no more than a mile off.
PHIL: Crikey dick, John. I can't figure you out. I think we could even see people on the deck.

> *They settle down.*

JIM: OK, can we get some sleep now?

Lights fade. There is the sound of a trickle in the darkness. A moment, then –

JOHN: Oh shit, oh dear! Oh shit! Oh dear! I may have just pissed in the garlic bottle.
RICK: *That* says it all.

It's the others' turn to laugh.

As the sun rises, JIM *emerges onto the hull.*

JIM: Early next morning I'm sitting staring at Great Barrier Island – dead ahead and the most beautiful thing I've seen in four months. The colour of it!

JOHN *comes up and sits beside* JIM, *also taking in the island.*

JOHN: Oh, my.
JIM, *looking at him, concerned after the previous night's trouble*: John, are you alright?
JOHN, *hesitating a moment, staring at Great Barrier, confusion on his face*: You know, I'm the kind of person who holds things inside. I got kind of carried away last night. I wasn't sure what I was going to do. I'm sorry.
JIM: You don't have to apologise to me, John.
JOHN, *looking down, pensive*: On the bulkhead over the dinette I had a photograph, do you remember, of my old boat off the beach on Moorea?
JIM: Yeah, I think so. Beautiful beach with palms, girl in a bikini and a guy sprawled on the sand. You?
JOHN: My brother David. I was behind the camera. Believe me, Jim, it was exactly what it looked like. The good life. I must have gazed at that picture a thousand times over the years. It always brought back happy memories. And dreams for

the future. I went looking for it on one of my dives. The frame was still there. But the photo was bleached completely white. Blank. (*He sighs, slumped and beaten.*)

Oh, I've lost everything. I have nothing left. At least you three have got something to go back to.

JIM: I'm really sorry, John. I know I've treated you like shit sometimes. And over the last month you've done a lot to keep my spirits up. You said the wreck of the *Rose-Noëlle* could be a turning point for me. Well, why not for you too, John? This could be just the start of something. A whole new beginning.

JOHN, *looking at him – a little sparkle rising into his eyes*: You're right, Jim. We're really lucky aren't we? Just look around.

JIM, *nodding*: We're the luckiest men in the Hauraki Gulf this morning. I reckon we just might be the luckiest men in the world!

> JOHN *grins, starts to sing a Tahitian love song. After a while,* RICK *comes up and looks at the island rising in front of them.*

RICK: We're going to land today.

> JOHN *nods.*

JIM: Alright!

RICK, *unable to completely share* JIM's *enthusiasm*: But this isn't going to be any party, you know.

> JIM *is sobered as he realises the danger they're going to face before the day is out.*

> *Sound: Rollers, surf breaking on rocks, growing louder –*

> PHIL *joins the others.*

PHIL: Look at those cliffs – and the rocks.

RICK: Let's face it, we'll be lucky if we get anywhere near the shore.

JIM: I think I can see a house up there on top of the hill.

JOHN: We have to stay with the boat as long as we can.

> *Joining the roar of surf is another sound, like fingernails being dragged down a blackboard.* JOHN *flinches as he listens.*

JIM: What's that?

JOHN: It's the mast. Hitting the seabed.

PHIL, *looking at* JOHN: I'm sorry about your boat, John.

> *Boom!* Rose-Noëlle *is picked up and dumped down with a shuddering crash. The air is full of noise and water.*

RICK: We're grounded on top of the rock.

> *The waves keep coming like freight trains, breaking over the crippled* Rose-Noëlle, *battering boat and men.*

PHIL: It's only a hundred yards to shore!

JOHN: Too far.

RICK: It's going to be dark soon. The boat's disintegrating around us. We have to make a move, and make it now!

JOHN: We need to make a raft of supplies and valuables. Only the essentials.

> *They each contribute.*

JIM: The two rolls of photos we took.

PHIL: Our food.

JOHN: My logbook.

RICK: My letters to Heather.

JOHN, *tying the last clove hitch*: Come on, Rick, let's get this thing launched!

> JOHN *and* RICK *move to launch the raft. As they do* –

PHIL: Look out!

> *Boom! A massive wave hits the boat, exploding round it, washing* JOHN *and* RICK *away.* RICK *clings to a rock, dazedly* –

JIM: Rick!

> – *before scrambling across to be hauled back up on the hull by* JIM *and* PHIL.

PHIL: We're off the rock! Heading for shore!

RICK: John!

JIM: Come on, John. Swim!

> RICK *picks up a rope, coils it, throws it towards* JOHN. *It lands just out of* JOHN'S *grasp.*

He's not even trying!

> RICK *throws again. The rope drops over the top of* JOHN *and he grabs it. They pull him in* –

PHIL: Come on, mate. Come on!

> – *and drag him on board. He's unable to help himself. He lies there, spent and gasping. With a decisive graunch the boat grounds once and for all.*

RICK: This is as close as we're going to get. Time to go!

> RICK *plunges in* – *followed by* JIM.

JIM: The water – up to our chests – is like lead. Pushing us forwards off-balance, then sucking us back. I'm sure the *Rose-Noëlle*'s going to come down on top of me and snuff me out.

PHIL: Come on, John.

> PHIL *plunges off the boat.* JOHN, *with his last reserves of strength, follows.*

JIM: One by one we make it to the two-metre ribbon of rocks which counts for a shoreline. Not dry land. Not even what I'd dignify with the word 'land' a few months ago. We're cold, numb, exhausted. But we're off the boat. And we're alive.

> JIM *huddles, blowing into his hands — but then (as the soundscape crossfades from exposed shoreline through birdsong to the interior of the bach) he unwinds, comfortable and warm from the mug he's holding in his hands.*

JIM: Coffee. Real coffee! After a night and a day lost in the bush, we finally find the bach we saw from the *Rose-Noëlle.*

> JIM *stays still as the others discover and break into the bach.*

RICK, *rattling the door*: Locked!
PHIL, *peering in the window*: Empty by the look of it.
JOHN, *reporting from the back*: There's a window round here we can climb through.

> JOHN, PHIL *and* RICK *clamber inside.*

JIM: Inside it's warm, dry —
JOHN: With chairs —
PHIL: And beds!
RICK, *disappointed*: It doesn't have a phone.
JIM: But it has a kitchen.

> *The others rifle through the cupboards, alternately mesmerised by the cornucopia — and eating like there's no tomorrow.*

JOHN: Muesli!
PHIL: Peanut butter!
RICK: Dried milk!
PHIL: Nuts – Marmite – honey –
JOHN: Biscuits – cereal –
RICK: Dried fruit – Milo –
JIM, *tears in his eyes*: It's over. Really over.

> *Sound: Rain is blown against the windows and rattles on the roof.*

RICK: Listen to that. If we were trying to come ashore now . . .
JIM: I look up the stairs and I see a vision. A strange man. Freshly shaven. Slim. Elegantly attired.
PHIL: Whose turn next in the bathroom?
JOHN: My God, Phillip –
JIM: You look a million bucks!
PHIL, *floating down, nonchalant*: Thanks, mate.
RICK: Where'd you get the slick threads?
PHIL: Wardrobe upstairs. There's plenty for the rest of you.
JIM: But we're not going to look as good as Phil. He's lost more weight than the rest of us. Forty, maybe fifty pounds. But on him it looks good, where it's skinny on me, and haggard on John and Rick. Phil the Hook Hofman – shallow water sailor, greedy fat boy, who we once talked about pushing off the boat as a liability – now looks around at us broken men with the trim vitality of someone returned from a health camp.
PHIL: What's for dinner?

> *Sound: Cross fade to Picton main street as –*

JIM, *amused*: Did I tell you, Rick? When I bumped into Phil in town, what he said about—

PHIL: Post-traumatic stress? Nah, never bothered me. I heard
you other jokers were seeing shrinks.

JIM: But not you, huh, Phil?

PHIL, *shrugging*: I slept easy, ate well, before I knew it it was like
I'd never been away.

> Well, maybe a few things different. For a while there,
Friday night in the pub, I was the one with the stories. And
of course Karen and me deciding it wasn't too late to have
another baby.

JIM: Philippa Rose.

PHIL: Yeah, she's corker, mate. Got a photo here somewhere . . .

JIM: I hear you finally finished that 'stone boat' of yours.

PHIL: Yep. Launched her. I've even taken the odd job delivering
yachts – right across the Pacific.

JIM, *shaking his head*: You amaze me, Phil. Even John reckons
he's finished with the sea. Never again.

PHIL, *shrugging*: Horses for courses. What happened didn't scare
me off. I reckon it even gave me a taste for it. A sort of a
sense of myself, you know?

JIM: Never underestimate the power of water.

PHIL: Right, Jim. That's right!

He claps JIM *on the shoulder and walks off.*

Sound reverts to bedroom.

JIM *turns back to the bed, and the farewell he's been dreading.*

JIM: It's nearly time. If I'm going to make that ferry . . .

RICK, *withdrawn*: Bit like John jumping out of the helicopter,
isn't it?

JIM: Breaking up the team?

RICK *doesn't answer.*

I don't want you to feel about me how you do about John.

RICK, *with an effort*: I don't. Course I don't.

JIM, *looking at him*: I wish you'd seen him again, Rick – that you'd come with me that time we were still in Auckland –

JOHN: Nice of you to visit, Jim.

JIM: – when he'd just come back from Great Barrier again.

JOHN: They wanted me to pick over the wreckage. There wasn't a piece I couldn't hold in one hand. Nothing worth salvaging. The valuables we floated ashore on the raft – my notes, bike-racing medals, photographs –

JIM: Rick's letters to Heather.

JOHN, *shaking his head*: Vanished. Torn apart and scattered by the sea. It didn't want me to bring anything back, Jim – not even a pair of shoes. (*He wiggles his bare feet and laughs.*)

Sound: Rocky shoreline, breakers –

JOHN: Though as I looked among the rocks, something did catch my eye – (JOHN *bends and picks up* –) a garland of plastic flowers. Given to me in the Islands twenty years before. A small thing, a fragile thing, all that was left of my life. (*He places the garland on his head.*) Forty-eight years old, standing in borrowed clothes on a beach inside the roar of the sea, wearing my life as lightly as a garland of flowers. (*He props on a piece of wreckage – and sings the Tahitian love song.*)

As the song continues, JIM *picks up his bags, moves them to the door.* RICK *watches him, but turns his head as* JIM *turns back.* JIM *comes back to the bed as* JOHN's *song ends.*

JIM: Rick? (RICK *doesn't respond, doesn't make it any easier.*) Say something, Rick.

RICK *summons the energy, grasps* JIM'*s hand, smiles –*

RICK: You just make sure you have a bloody amazing time, mate.

JIM: I wish—

RICK: No – I wish I could tell you what it's meant to me to have you here the past eight months. You're the best friend a guy could have. (*He and* JIM *embrace, neither wanting to be first to let go.*) Always been lousy at goodbyes. I'm trying to get better.

JIM *stands up, knowing it will be the last time he will see* RICK. *He steps back.*

Happy trails, Jim.

JIM: You too, Rick.

Music up as JIM *backs away, leaving* RICK *in a pool of light. They hold each other's eyes before the contact is broken as* JIM *turns front.*

It was a few weeks later, Heather called to tell me. I stood looking out the window at the sea off Cape Cod . . . and I thought of the Sounds. Early morning – no one for miles – Rick slips the kayak into the water . . .

RICK *overlaps, then takes over, his speech clearing and his 'frozen' right side thawing until he is restored to full movement.*

RICK: I slip the kayak into the water, slide into the cockpit and I'm arrowing out across a sea of glass. No sound but the drip of water from the paddle blade. Shoulders feel good as I flex, dig deep . . . (*He looks up.*) Sun's coming up. Start of a breeze. I've got the whole day ahead of me. (*He paddles on strongly as the light on him fades.*)

 Pause.

JIM: When we first got off the *Rose-Noëlle* I asked Rick if he felt humbled by the whole experience. He looked at me like I must be mad – and just said, 'Shit no!' (*He shakes his head.*)

 Stubborn. But I know I couldn't have survived without my friend's courage and determination, his hand in mine telling me always that he wouldn't let me fall – for all his sometimes pig-headedness which was just the flipside of his strength.

 We were all flawed. But thank God they were different flaws. Sometimes I think if you took the four of us apart – separated out all the strengths and the weaknesses, what was stupid and wise, heroic and generous and petty and selfish – and used the bits and pieces to make two men . . . God, what a sorry excuse for a human being one of them would be. A panicky, pompous, high-handed, low-initiative, argumentative dickhead. Someone you wouldn't want to be in an elevator with for thirty seconds, never mind four months on a capsized boat.

 But the other guy, made up of the best bits of ourselves, I think I know what he'd be like – from moments when I was sure I'd glimpsed him.

PHIL: What's for dinner?

The dinner scene takes up where it left off earlier, music in quietly as they move around, reverently setting up the table.

JIM: The best linen.

PHIL: Personal table napkins.

JOHN: The bach's finest silver.
RICK: Candles.

> *Lights down to candlelight.* PHIL *holds up two bottles of wine.*

PHIL: The red or the white, gentlemen?
JIM, *cooking*: It's Italian. Spaghetti with asparagus.
JOHN: Then the red of course.

> PHIL *uncorks it.* RICK *brings glasses.*

RICK: The family crystal.

> PHIL *pours.* RICK *lifts a glass of wine by its stem and holds it to the candlelight.*

JOHN: Beautiful.

> JIM *brings the bowl of spaghetti, hot and fresh and places it in the middle of the table – a sacred offering.*

RICK: Sit down, Jim.
JIM: I'll just get the Parmesan.

> *They sit, hesitate – united.*

I'd just like to say – that there's nowhere else I want to be right now but here.

> *The others nod.*

JOHN: Well, aren't we having fun?

> RICK *smiles at* JOHN.

RICK: Yeah. Yeah, John. We're having fun.

> PHIL *lifts his glass.*

PHIL: Cheers.

They join him in the toast, saluting each other.

ALL: Cheers.

Lights fade as they begin the meal.

The End.

TRICK OF THE LIGHT

Introduction

Trick of the Light is a puzzle box. Like all good puzzles it can be turned this way or that – you can start at any corner to find your way into the middle. Looking at it, I see the play as a conjunction of a number of interests or obsessions of mine, which reflect and refract each other.

Working backwards (as befits the play), there's the Thomas case and how it marked a turning point in our history. The way New Zealanders split over the issue – and the different kinds of people who lined up on either side – announced a sea change in our culture and prefigured the explosion of the '81 Springbok tour. In particular it affected our relationship with the police, which lurched into the zone of a marriage gone bad following one infidelity. Nothing could be quite the same once the trust was lost.

Then there is the enduring mystery of the crime behind the Thomas trials, the Crewe murders; and the nature of mystery itself, our urge to populate the unknowable, to fill the vacuum. And what we fill it with: ourselves – our own experience, our view of life. We surround questions with facts that we would love to be evidence but are only clues which can be interpreted this way or that, depending on where you're standing or who you are. Especially tantalising to me, is the idea that there is a female and a male way of looking at the Crewe murders. Because . . .

I wanted to write about men and women, the different way they perceive the world. I wanted to look at gender: what has changed over the last thirty years and what has stayed the same. I read a quote somewhere: 'Any marriage is more interesting than any murder.' What if the two were intertwined? What if a marriage might hold the solution to a murder, or a murder reverberate far enough to kill a marriage, separate a family?

And (we're there) it was the idea of family that came first. I've always been fascinated with what is passed down from

parents to children, genetically and otherwise. From this came
the basic structure for the play: two generations of a family
– with obvious doubling of mother/daughter and father/son
– but with the twist that the daughter's personality takes after
her father and vice versa, presenting a challenge to the actors
to swap personas halfway through. How might the same basic
personality manifest itself differently in a man and a woman? In
Trick of the Light the third character became the converse of this
– the same person who only looks different in the two halves of
the play.

An influence on the setting was no doubt a motel on the
shores of Lake Taupo where I once spent a long night. I still
shake my head every time I pass its decaying sign. In the first
production of *Trick of the Light* at Circa Theatre, Andrew Foster
brilliantly realised the concrete block claustrophobia of this and
every other vintage kiwi motel unit.

Trick of the Light has turned out to be the second of
(currently) four plays in a row I've written about parents and
children. Hardly surprising given that in a single generation
the norm of Mum, Dad and the kids has become a much
more complicated and fractured proposition. We're still trying
to catch up and count the cost – me included. Consequently
there's sadness here, and separation, but balanced by a sense of
reconciliation and hope. Hope is something I believe the end
of every story should have. Otherwise why bother? It's just that
Trick of the Light, being what it is, ends in the middle.

First Performance

Trick of the Light was first performed at Circa Theatre, Wellington, on 28 September 2002, with the following cast:

BEVAN:	Sean Allan
CLARE:	Michele Amas
MRS WICKS:	Toby Leach
JAN:	Michele Amas
TOM:	Sean Allan
PHILLIP:	Toby Leach

Director	Katherine McRae
Design	Andrew Foster
Costume Design	Janet Dunn
Costume Assistant	Noeline Anderson
Sound Design	Jeremy Cullen at Marmalade Audio
Lighting Design	Martyn Roberts and Juliette Howard
Stage Manager	Robert Ormsby
Technical Operator	Marcus McShane
Publicity	Marjorie McKee
Graphic Design	base2
Photography	Stephen A'Court
Consultant	Colin McLean
Set	Iain Cooper, John Hodgkins, Chris Clements
House Manager	Suzanne Blackburn
Front of House	Linda Wilson

Characters

BEVAN:	– 38
CLARE:	– 40
MRS WICKS:	– early 60s
JAN:	– 34
TOM:	– 36
PHILLIP:	– a young man

Note:
Trick of the Light is performed by three actors. The roles are doubled as follows: BEVAN/TOM, CLARE/JAN, MRS WICKS/PHILLIP.

Setting

Unit Five – the Midway Motel, 2003. A tacky, concrete-block, 60s construction, the motel unit contains: a kitchenette (with louvre windows), a small formica dining table with three chairs (an opened out newspaper parcel of old fish and chips on it), a couple of ugly armchairs. Some interestingly ugly prints hang round the cream-painted concrete walls. There is a stillness on everything, something like a museum piece, or Tutankhamen's Tomb – a place perfectly preserved from a time past. The curtains are closed, the fabric faded and rotted where the sun has touched them. Before the play starts there is light repeatedly growing and fading outside, shadows travelling, as if days, nights and seasons are passing outside.

Trick

'Do It Again' by Steely Dan plays as the lights go down to darkness. There is the amplified sound of a rifle bolt slammed home, a reverberating gunshot, the amplified sound of the bolt pulled back and the 'spring' of the cartridge case being ejected.

The lights go up on a late afternoon in winter. The last light is fading. There is the noise of birds in the trees outside. MRS WICKS *is silhouetted against the window as she stands on a chair finishing taking down the curtains. She appears to be a woman in her early 60s who, when she climbs down to fold the last curtain, walks with a slight limp. She is in stockinged feet, having slipped her shoes off before climbing on the chair. She dumps the folded curtains out of sight in a cupboard she has to yank open.*

BEVAN, *off*: Hello!

> MRS WICKS *jumps. Glimpsing* BEVAN *through the window, she panics and ducks down.*

Hello? Anyone there?

> BEVAN *appears in the open doorway, carrying an overnight bag. He looks round and sniffs at the slightly strange atmosphere. He hits the light switch by the door – and the bulb promptly blows with a metallic pop.*

BEVAN: Bang!

> MRS WICKS *springs up.*

Oh, hello.
MRS WICKS: Yes?
BEVAN: I've just blown your bulb. Or is it my bulb? For the night.

MRS WICKS *gazes at him in alarm.* BEVAN, *38 years old but still somehow boyish, glances round the dim still life of the motel unit.*

This is number five?

MRS WICKS: It's meant to be tomorrow.

BEVAN: Tomorrow?

MRS WICKS: Friday. The ninth.

BEVAN: No, Thursday. Today. (*He checks his watch.*) The eighth.

MRS WICKS *stares at him in horror.*

It was you I talked to on the phone? About booking Unit Five?

MRS WICKS: It's not ready.

BEVAN: I don't mind roughing it.

MRS WICKS: I could put you somewhere else.

BEVAN: I particularly wanted five.

MRS WICKS: I can put you up in the house.

BEVAN: Your house?

MRS WICKS: It's comfortable.

BEVAN: What about the other units?

MRS WICKS: They're . . . all full up.

BEVAN: You're full? There's no other cars.

MRS WICKS: Not everyone's got a car.

BEVAN: I thought that was the point of a motel. Motor hotel. Must be odd to see people walk up, stay the night then walk off again in the morning. Specially out here.

MRS WICKS: I'll show you the bedrooms. They get lovely morning sun. (*Slipping on her shoes, she tries to usher him out.*)

BEVAN: Nice shoes.

She looks down at them.

My mother had a pair like that. It's because of her I'm here. Actually.

Mrs Wicks: We could all say that.

Bevan: Sorry?

Mrs Wicks: It's thanks to your mother you're here.

Bevan, *grinning*: I suppose! (*He looks at* Mrs Wicks.) I guess it sounds a bit strange – but as I said on the phone we're really set on having this one. Number five.

> *As he casts an interested glance around – showing no sign of leaving –* Mrs Wicks *becomes perturbed.*

If this is number five? There's nothing on the door.

Mrs Wicks: No.

Bevan: How do people find it?

Mrs Wicks: Quite comfortable.

> *Anxious to hide something, she positions herself –*

Bevan: Perhaps they just look for the one without the number.

> *– to move an armchair to cover something on the floor.*

Mrs Wicks: Yes. Five's got no number. As long as you remember that.

Bevan: It doesn't really need to be five, then, does it?

Mrs Wicks: I'm sorry?

Bevan: I mean without a number who's to say it's Unit Five of the Midway Motel? It could be the Presidential Suite. The Honeymoon Arbor. The Jungle Room.

> *As* Bevan *heads for the table,* Mrs Wicks *hurriedly scrunches up the newspaper on it into a tight parcel.*

Look, don't worry about tidying up.

Mrs Wicks, *dropping the newspaper in a kitchen bin*: It's not suitable. I've taken the curtains down.

Bevan: More light in the morning.

Mrs Wicks: The house is very warm.

BEVAN: I'll be fine here. Really.

MRS WICKS: Isn't your sister with you?

BEVAN: My sister?

MRS WICKS: You said on the phone there were two of you coming. A woman.

BEVAN: I don't remember saying she was my sister.

MRS WICKS: I just assumed.

BEVAN: That if I was staying in a motel with a woman, she must be my sister?

MRS WICKS: You had the same last name.

BEVAN: I would've assumed she was my wife. If I was you.

MRS WICKS: I'll get another bulb. From the house.

> MRS WICKS *heads for the door.* BEVAN *has his back to her. She stops and looks at* BEVAN *as if she's summoning her courage to say something. Unnoticing,* BEVAN *gets in first.*

BEVAN: Where exactly did the shooting happen?

> MRS WICKS *stops dead, stares at him.*

BEVAN: Suppose you just want to forget about it. Not very good for business.

> MRS WICKS *is still looking stunned.*

On the other hand, I bet everyone who comes through still asks you about it. Even after thirty years. I guess every place has to be famous for something. And round here it's the Thomas Case.

> *Awareness has gradually been dawning on* MRS WICKS.

MRS WICKS: The murders? Oh no, that wasn't round here.

BEVAN: No?

MRS WICKS: No. Away over there that was. Five miles. Easily.

BEVAN: You were here at the time?

MRS WICKS: I've lived here all my life.

BEVAN: Just you and your son, is it? (*No reply.*) I noticed on the sign it said 'and Son'.

MRS WICKS: He's – not here any more.

> *Short awkward pause. Again* MRS WICKS *seems about to say something. Unfortunately so does* BEVAN. *They speak together.*

The thing is, you see, I knew—

BEVAN: Look, I wondered if you might've known— (*They stop.*) Sorry. After you.

MRS WICKS, *summoning her courage*: Well, what I was going to say—

> BEVAN'*s mobile starts to ring.*

BEVAN: Whoops.

> *As he fishes the phone out of his pocket –*

MRS WICKS: I'll get you that bulb. (*She casts a glance round the room.*) I might bring two.

> *She hurries out.* BEVAN *checks the incoming number on the display before answering.*

BEVAN: Thanks for making me look like a townie wanker.

> *Pause.*

I knew you'd change your mind. I knew you couldn't keep away.

> *Pause.*

You've gone past it. No, if you've hit the main road you must have passed it. Do a U-ey and come back. It's only about a minute. (*He walks around the room as he talks, idly examining things.*) Not what I'd call well advertised. There's a sign but it's sort of lying in a ditch.

Pause.

Well try going slower this time. Half a million k.

He picks up something on the mantelpiece, looks at the perfect pattern in the thin layer of dust underneath it.

BEVAN, *in response to* CLARE's *question*: Probably a bit different to your usual accommodation.

He notices a picture hanging slightly crooked. He adjusts it, revealing a slice of strikingly unfaded wallpaper.

No, I've only been here five minutes. I was just going to ask about Mum when you called.

He unhooks the picture and takes it down. Behind is a skewed square of original-colour wallpaper.

Got it? Great. See you in a sec.
    (*Afterthought*) Oh, it's the one with no number. The unit formerly known as five.

BEVAN grins, turns the phone off and pockets it. He hangs the picture back up, tilting it carefully to fit its 'shadow'. He unzips his bag and carefully removes something wrapped in underwear. He peels off the socks and boxer shorts to reveal an urn.

He 'shows' the room to the urn.

Here you go then. See anything you recognise? Care to share it with the rest of us?

He stands the urn on the table. He drops his bag onto an armchair – which puffs out dust like a bellows. BEVAN observes this a moment, then notices the deep indentations in the carpet left by the armchair Mrs Wicks *moved. He scuffs at them with his foot. He's just about to move the chair back to see if its legs fit the marks when* Clare *comes in with an armload of lightbulbs. She takes in the surroundings at a glance.*

Clare: No. (*She goes out again.*)
Bevan: Clare!

> Clare *comes back to dump the lightbulbs.*

Clare: No way. Look at this place!
Bevan: Pretty intriguing, eh?
Clare: It's got no curtains.
Bevan: Hasn't been done up in a while.
Clare: You can't stay in a place with no curtains!
Bevan: One night. That's all.

> Clare – *40, well dressed, driven, and at this point wound-up – looks at him.*

Clare: I'm out of here, Bevan. I'm telling you.
Bevan: Fine.
Clare, *sniffing*: It's musty. (*She runs a finger along a chair.*) Filthy.
Bevan: She said it wasn't ready.
Clare: And it's creepy. With Mrs Danvers out there.
Bevan: I thought her name was Wicks.
Clare: Mrs Danvers! Out of *Rebecca*.
Bevan: Sounds like a racehorse. She wasn't expecting us till tomorrow. She got the date wrong.
Clare, *glancing sharply at him*: She did?
Bevan: That's what I said.
Clare: Where'd she get the idea I was your wife?
Bevan: Eh?

CLARE: 'Your husband's already here.'

BEVAN: Not from me. In fact marriage seemed to be the last thing she assumed.

CLARE: Oh no.

BEVAN: What?

CLARE: It's some ghastly shack-up place!

BEVAN: Here?

CLARE: Farmers with their bit of totty from the city. I bet during the Agricultural Field Days they rent rooms by the hour! Oh God. (*She looks at her hand.*)

BEVAN: What?

CLARE: No wedding ring.

BEVAN: You told her, didn't you? When she called me your husband?

CLARE: It took me by surprise.

BEVAN: What did you say?

CLARE: I just thought – for a second . . . I don't know what I thought!

BEVAN: That Gavin might be here?

CLARE: The way she was staring at me. Then she's loading me up with lightbulbs!

BEVAN: A bulb blew.

CLARE: What do we need four for?

BEVAN: 'We' don't. If you're not staying.

CLARE: I'm not. I'm not, Bevan. I don't care what you say.

BEVAN, *shrugging*: Fine.

CLARE: This is so typical. It's so simple for other people isn't it? You just scatter them. A hill overlooking the sea. Off the stern of a yacht. A favourite rose bush. (CLARE *has avoided looking at the urn until now. She almost speaks to it.*) Just to do one thing. To die like an ordinary person.

BEVAN: So what do you think? Now you've seen it?

CLARE: I don't even want to think.

BEVAN: Where's your fascination with mystery?

CLARE: The less I think the better.

BEVAN, *scoffing at the implication*: Oh, come on. Some grubby weekend? Mum?

CLARE, *picking up boxer shorts*: What's this?

BEVAN: I had to pack her in so she wouldn't break.

CLARE: In your underwear?

BEVAN: And socks. They're clean. (*He gets a chair and stands on it to change the lightbulb.*) I'll tell her you're my sister. Next time I see her I'll say, 'My sister and I.' 'My sister had to leave.' 'My sister.'

CLARE: Not like that. That'd be worse than saying nothing.

BEVAN: Switch.

> *She flicks the switch by the door. The light comes on.* BEVAN *climbs down.*

CLARE: Why is it people think they can get anything they want from other people just by dying? I mean what is this whole 'last wishes' 'final bequest' thing? Why, just because they're dead, do we suddenly have to bow to their every demand?

> BEVAN *has pulled the keys out of the door in order to close it. As he drops the keys on the table, he feels something greasy on his fingers. He sniffs them.*

BEVAN: CRC.

CLARE: What?

BEVAN: In the lock. It's not because she's dead. I thought. It's because she's our mother.

CLARE: Don't lecture me.

BEVAN: I'm not lecturing you.

CLARE: Don't give me that 'our mother'. She was my mother too.

BEVAN: That's what I said. 'Our' mother. Yours and mine.

CLARE: You don't really want to stay here. You're doing it to get at me.

BEVAN: Clare.

CLARE: You want me to feel guilty. As if I'd be letting her down by refusing to go along with this bizarre whim!

BEVAN: Look, Clare, she's dead. She's cremated. She's – dust in a bottle. For all we know it's not even her in there!

CLARE: Eh?

BEVAN: So she's not going to know the difference. If you want to go, then go.

CLARE: Why should I?

BEVAN: What?

CLARE: Why should I have to be the one to go? I don't want to be that person any more!

BEVAN: What person?

CLARE: Constable Clare coming in to break up the party for you and Mum. She's dead, but you still have to be the indulgent one – think it's all a bit of a laugh, an intriguing mystery – and leave it up to me to say, 'This is ridiculous!' Well, I'm not going to do it any more, Bevan. It's time you took a turn.

BEVAN: I'm fine here.

CLARE: Admit this is a waste of time – and then we can both go.

BEVAN: I'm finding the whole thing fascinating.

CLARE: So this is how it's going to be, is it?

BEVAN: How what's going to be?

CLARE: When we see each other. For the rest of our lives am I going to have to be the parent?

BEVAN: What are you talking about?

CLARE: I'm talking about this! 'I want to spend the night in Unit Five of the Mountain View Motel.' Some morphine-crazed fantasy she'd probably forgotten two minutes later.

BEVAN: She wrote it down.

CLARE: And you had to make something of it. You had to decide it was her last request.

BEVAN: She wasn't that drugged up.

CLARE: She was on that pump thing!

BEVAN: She was lucid when she told me about this place. She was absolutely herself.

CLARE: How do you know?

BEVAN: I was there.

CLARE: Don't you dare. Don't you dare throw that at me.

BEVAN: I'm not throwing anything. You're the one starting with all this 'parent' crap. I'm thirty-eight years old. I haven't needed a parent in a long time. Which is pretty lucky, since I've got one in a bottle and one on the Gold Coast.

CLARE: He would be here if he could travel.

BEVAN: He'd be here if his wife would let him.

CLARE: He's had a bypass!

BEVAN: Six months ago. (*He takes a breath.*) Look – you're in Sydney, I'm in Wellington – we hardly ever see each other. You get on the plane tomorrow and we can go back to that.

CLARE: What are you saying? That I don't want to see you?

BEVAN: No.

CLARE: What sort of thing is that to say?

BEVAN: All I'm saying is considering the slim amount of time we spend together I don't know where you're getting this 'parent' thing from.

CLARE: It's you who never calls. I get a Christmas card one year in three.

BEVAN: So does everyone else.

CLARE: I'm not everyone else. I'm your sister!

BEVAN: Yeah, well at least when you do get a card it's a bit more personal. Not those ticker-tape news headlines you flash across yours. 'Katy lost 4 teeth', 'Tamsin prize at school', 'Rarotonga v dot relaxing'.

CLARE: That's not fair!

BEVAN: They're produced by production line.

CLARE: It's a big job. I have to start in November.

BEVAN: Admit it, Clare, you've got three phrases and you rotate them!

Pained, CLARE *flaps about making a noise.*

What?

CLARE: I want to cry and there's nowhere clean to do it!

BEVAN: Here.

BEVAN *puts his jacket on a chair.* CLARE *sits on it and cries.* BEVAN *watches her for a while. He wonders if he should put his arm around her, but doesn't.*

And it's Midway.

CLARE, *sniffing*: What?

BEVAN: You said Mountain View. It's the Midway Motel.

CLARE, *blowing her nose*: I need a cigarette. (*As she gets cigarette and lighter from her bag –*) I suppose I saw the mountain.

BEVAN: What mountain?

CLARE: Oh for God's sake, Bevan. I know men aren't supposed to be able to find anything.

CLARE *crosses to the door and opens it. She lights up and stands in the doorway smoking and looking out.*

BEVAN: You can probably smoke in here.

CLARE: It's a habit now. Besides there's no ashtray.

BEVAN *proffers the urn.*

Very funny.

BEVAN: Ashes to ashes.

Pause.

CLARE: Of course it's her.

BEVAN: Eh?

CLARE: You saying it might not even be her. Of course it's her.

BEVAN: How do we know?

CLARE: Just don't, Bevan.

BEVAN: Well it's a fact isn't it? We can never be one hundred per cent sure.

CLARE: It's a reputable firm not some bunch of cowboys.

BEVAN: How do we know they don't do them in batches then just divide up what's left?

CLARE: Well obviously.

Pause.

BEVAN: Obviously what?

CLARE: I said don't. Don't start.

BEVAN: Fine. We can never be sure. That's fine.

CLARE: We can be sure because it's a reputable firm who were contracted to cremate our mother and put her ashes in that urn and because sometimes things are exactly what they say they are!

Pause.

BEVAN: That's a touching faith.

CLARE: Jesus, Mary and Joseph.

Pause.

BEVAN: I thought it went off OK. In the end.

CLARE: I didn't know half the people there. (*She considers.*) But it was nice. (*Remembers.*) What was the idea of 'Morning Has Broken'?

BEVAN, *shrugging*: I couldn't think what she liked. So I just picked off their list. The Crematorium Hot One Hundred.

CLARE: I never heard her play Cat Stevens in her life.

BEVAN: What do you think would have been more appropriate? 'Light My Fire'? 'Disco Inferno'?

CLARE *also draws a bit of a blank.*

CLARE: Something by John Denver? She liked him, didn't she?

BEVAN: Did she?

Pause.

It was sweet, though. The way everyone talked about Mum.
Some of those old ladies didn't want to go home, did they?
CLARE: I still hate them. Funerals. I hate sitting there wondering
what mine'll be like. Who'll turn up.
BEVAN: Don't worry. I'll be there.
CLARE: You'll be long gone.
BEVAN: You're the oldest.
CLARE: You're a man.
BEVAN: You're a smoker.
CLARE: And Dad's the one with heart disease. Are you having
check-ups?
BEVAN: He could have come.
CLARE: Not according to Fiona.

Pause.

BEVAN: I was a bit surprised you didn't bring the girls.
CLARE: I knew it'd be a mad rush getting on the plane, then
organising everything here. They saw her at Christmas
– that's the important thing.
BEVAN: Mum said they were lovely.
CLARE: They were with her. (*She sighs.*) Usually they're so –
uninterested in everything. I don't know if it's a response
or not.
BEVAN: To you and Gavin?
CLARE: Half the kids they know are shuttled between parents
on weekends. Separation and divorce – it's a Surry Hills
coming of age ritual. Get your first period, watch your
parents split.
BEVAN: It's been a year, I guess they've got used to it.
CLARE: They seemed used to it from day one. From Ground
Zero.

BEVAN: I thought Gavin might come too.

CLARE: What for?

BEVAN: It's not like he didn't know Mum. (*He shrugs.*) I don't know – for the sake of the girls. To support you.

CLARE: This is just a wild guess, Bevan, but if he wanted to support me, I don't think he'd have left, do you?

BEVAN: Our family's shrinking.

CLARE: Don't look at me. I've done my bit.

BEVAN: Lucky Mum had plenty of friends.

CLARE: Why didn't she get a busload of them to whisk her off on this tragical mystery tour?

BEVAN: She wanted us to do it.

CLARE: To do what? Prop her on the table for the night? Why?

BEVAN: This place meant something to her.

CLARE: It's pretty obvious what.

> *She finishes her cigarette and comes back in.*

BEVAN: What's obvious?

CLARE: I need to clean my teeth.

> *She takes a travelling toothbrush out of her handbag.*

BEVAN: You still do that?

CLARE: Smoking I could kick, it's the toothbrushing that's addictive.

BEVAN: What's so obvious?

CLARE: Remember all those little holidays she took, her regular away trips, when you'd come to Dad and me?

BEVAN: She stayed with friends.

CLARE: Which friends?

> BEVAN *thinks then shrugs.*

She'd ring up – but I was never sure exactly where she was ringing from. Were you?

BEVAN: Even if she was coming here with someone – why would she bother to hide it?

CLARE: For the sake of her 'special' friend?

BEVAN: Some guy who was married? Mum – a scarlet woman? I don't see it.

CLARE: Ever heard of Occam's Razor? It's a deductive technique. We did it in law. It says that all things being equal, the simplest explanation that fits the facts is usually the right one.

BEVAN: On the other hand you can simply be wrong.

CLARE: Why else would you shack up in a place like this? The only thing it's got going for it is that there's nobody for miles around. I knew as soon as I saw it. I've known it for years. You don't just walk out on someone like she did to Dad. And never explain it.

BEVAN: What's to explain?

CLARE: I beg your pardon?

BEVAN: They grew apart.

CLARE, *scoffing*: Grew apart? That's like blaming a plane crash on gravity.

Those 'holidays' of hers started way before she and Dad split up. Do you remember that? And how Dad would be in an absolutely foul mood the whole time she was away? (*She looks round.*) Ugh. The whole thing's so squalid.

BEVAN: I don't buy it.

CLARE: She never could do anything wrong by you.

CLARE *heads for the bathroom.*

BEVAN: If you were so sure she was up to something, why didn't you ask her?

CLARE, *stopping*: I did.

BEVAN: When?

CLARE: I don't know – sometime in the year after she left. It was in that depressing flat of hers – I remember that much. She was packing and I accused her of going to meet her lover.

BEVAN: What'd she say?

CLARE: She laughed. Said she was going to spend a few days with a friend.

BEVAN: Mr Whatsit with the razor might say that was the simplest explanation.

CLARE: Except I asked her about this friend. Who was it? A woman or a man? She suddenly seemed to be absorbed in her packing. She had this little mysterious smile on her face. So I asked again. Is it a woman? Or is it a man? Then she said it, Bevan. The three words that go together to make the most guilty phrase in the English language. Just a friend. (*She looks at* BEVAN.) Just – a – friend.

BEVAN: So that's it? The most damning evidence you've got? It's not exactly a photo of her in bed with some guy. (*He shudders at the thought.*)

CLARE: Oh, is this making you feel uncomfortable, Bevan? Well you can take a number and stand in line. I've felt uncomfortable about it for years while you've had your head buried in the sand.

BEVAN: Oh, come on. Mum cheating? Sneaking around? Both before and after she broke up with Dad?

CLARE: What other explanation can you put on it? Or on this? Except that it's some last tawdry flyby – a final salute to the grubby sex that meant more to her than Dad or we did. And just to absolutely put the seal on it she gets us, her own children, to be the bearers of her torch – (*picking up the urn and brandishing it*) – in tribute to the extramarital, homewrecking, bed-hopping Olympics of yesteryear!

BEVAN: Would you mind putting Mum down?

CLARE, *waving the urn*: Why? If she ends up scattered round here – all the better isn't it? That's what she wanted. To breathe the dust of passion past one last time, take a final roll on the faded carpet of desire!

BEVAN *takes the urn off her and places it back on the table. Pause.*

BEVAN: So that's the only explanation, is it?

CLARE *cocks an eyebrow.*

The only reason anyone would stay out here in the middle of nowhere. Because they didn't want to be caught doing what they were doing. (*He looks at her.*) What if this wasn't the middle of nowhere? What if at one time it was quite handy – even the nearest motel – to somewhere?

CLARE, *gazing at him*: Go on.

BEVAN: When I was about eight, so that makes you ten, Mum and Dad went away for a few days. You remember?

CLARE: No.

BEVAN: We stayed at Nana and Grandad's. It was when I knocked over that vase and the water went down the back of their TV and blew it up.

CLARE: And you blamed it on the cat.

BEVAN: Do you know where they went?

CLARE: I can barely remember *that* they went.

BEVAN: Dad said it was work. I asked why I couldn't go.

CLARE: He took Mum with him on police business?

BEVAN: It wasn't long after he joined HQ. Maybe he wanted to show her the perks of the new job.

CLARE, *sceptical*: By bringing her here?

BEVAN: I did a little research. We're talking 1973, right?

CLARE: So?

BEVAN: The Thomas Case.

CLARE: The Thomas Case?

BEVAN: It was round here. A few miles up the road.

CLARE: Is this another one of your conspiracy theories?

BEVAN: We'd just gone back to school – so it would've been the beginning of the year. Right before Thomas's second trial.

CLARE: Dad had nothing to do with the Thomas Case.

BEVAN: How do you know?

CLARE: He would have said.

BEVAN: No he wouldn't.

CLARE: Then how do you know he did?

BEVAN: Because he'd never talk about it.

> CLARE *just looks at him.*

Even when it was in all the papers, front page, he wouldn't talk about it.

CLARE: Can you remember him ever talking about anything to do with work?

BEVAN: OK. But Mum didn't talk about it either.

CLARE: Mum? What would she want to talk about the Thomas Case for?

BEVAN: Except once. Round the time Thomas was finally pardoned. I said something about who did do it then? Mum sat me down and gave me chapter and verse on the murder–suicide theory. And believe me, she knew what she was talking about, she had it all down.

CLARE: The what theory?

BEVAN: That it was an inside job. The wife shot her husband, then got her father involved in dumping his body. But she couldn't face what she'd done – and killed herself a few days later. So the sighting of the woman at the gate was actually her – in between shooting her husband and shooting herself.

CLARE: What woman? What gate?

BEVAN: What'd they teach you in law?

CLARE: Contracts. Torts.

BEVAN: Know your murders, Clare. It's our heritage in this country. Anyway, the story goes on with her father getting rid of her body as well so he wouldn't get blamed for the whole mess. But what I remember is how Mum talked about

it. Like it was important to her – or at least important that
I listened.

CLARE: I worry about you, Bevan. Are you going to become an
old man in urine-stained corduroys who mutters to himself
at bus stops?

BEVAN: Then there was the postcard. They sent me a postcard
on that trip. From Hamilton. It said they were just passing
through, and they'd send you one from Auckland. But you
never got it.

CLARE: I never got it?

BEVAN: Your postcard never came.

CLARE: How can you possibly remember that?

BEVAN: Because it was the only time I got something and you
didn't get one too.

CLARE: Maybe they were just having too good a time.

BEVAN: Or maybe she hated you.

CLARE: Maybe you're adopted.

BEVAN: Maybe she found you at the zoo.

CLARE: So this mysteriously absent postcard implies what,
according to you?

BEVAN: They didn't get to Auckland. Something cut their trip
short.

CLARE: Something which happened here?

BEVAN: This unit in this motel has some kind of significance.
To Mum at least. Plus Dad said it was work. And back then
the most important police work in the country was just
over there-a-ways.

CLARE: Why does that make her want to come back here after
she's dead?

BEVAN: What if they found something out?

CLARE: 'They'?

BEVAN: Some information about the case.

CLARE: This is Mum and Dad here, Bevan. Not some husband-
and-wife crime-fighting duo.

BEVAN: It could have been something to do with the police case against Thomas. Something they couldn't talk about.

CLARE: Are you saying Mum and Dad framed Arthur Allan Thomas?

BEVAN: Now you're being ridiculous.

CLARE: *I* am?

BEVAN: I'm just saying they could've . . .

CLARE: What?

BEVAN: I don't know!

CLARE *imitates a muttering old man at the bus stop.*

What about Dad quitting the job like he did?

CLARE: That was years later.

BEVAN: I bumped into Barry Sewell a while back. His old man told him there was a whisper that Dad was involved in some kind of cover-up.

CLARE: A what?

BEVAN: Something about a shooting. Said it was hushed up.

CLARE: A shooting?

BEVAN: That was the story he got.

CLARE: Absolute garbage.

BEVAN: How do you know?

CLARE: That's rubbish, Bevan! It was politics. HQ politics. The Commissioner took a set against him. Over some report.

BEVAN: I never heard about any report.

CLARE: Dad said he gave them the report in good faith. When it came back to bite them on the bum they decided they needed a scapegoat.

BEVAN: What about what Barry told me?

CLARE, *pacing*: That is so you. Always convinced there's something going on. That all you have to do is undo some tangled knot of conspiracy, and it'll explain everything. It'll put the universe back on its axis for you. Well it won't, Bevan.

BEVAN: What's that supposed to mean?

CLARE, *frustrated*: I don't know what I'm even doing here!

BEVAN: What *are* you doing here? Yesterday at the funeral you said no way.

CLARE: I just thought, crazily, that she might be trying to tell me something. Us something.

BEVAN: What?

CLARE: She might be attempting, at last, to explain. And instead what do I get? The usual wall of silence from her – and you raving about some long-extinct murder trial. What's the Thomas Case got to do with us? That's not going to explain why she upped and walked out! Why she split this family right down the middle!

BEVAN: Who's talking about that?

CLARE: I am!

BEVAN: I thought we were talking about why Mum wanted to come back here?

CLARE: You don't *see* anything, do you? The real mystery, the real impenetrably deep, impossible-to-solve mystery, isn't who shot someone. It's what goes on between two people. Round a dining table, in a bed, in a marriage.

BEVAN: Mum and Dad?

CLARE: Dad and Mum. Me and Gavin. Unravel that mystery for me. And don't tell me 'you just grow apart'.

BEVAN: You must know why you and Gavin split up.

CLARE: We didn't split up. He walked out.

BEVAN: Like Mum.

CLARE: We get left, Bevan.

BEVAN: I don't.

CLARE: You're never with anyone long enough.

BEVAN: And you think that's deliberate. So I won't repeat the tragic example of my parents.

CLARE: No doubt you've got another explanation.

BEVAN: Are you telling me Gavin left out of a clear blue sky?

CLARE: Marriages aren't clear blue skies. They have cloudy patches, moderate to heavy rainfall, overnight frost in the ranges. That doesn't explain why some end one morning and others just sail on.

BEVAN: You must have asked him. He must have said something.

CLARE: Of course I asked him! Of course he said something! Just like I asked Mum. It's nearly driven me mad with frustration that neither of them made any sense!

BEVAN: You are, aren't you? You're one of these people who blames everything on their parents breaking up.

CLARE *turns away.*

Look, all I know is that feelings change. There's nothing inexplicable about that.

CLARE: I didn't see any change. What changed?

BEVAN: How do I know, Clare? I wasn't there.

CLARE: You were when it was Mum and Dad. I don't think their feelings changed.

BEVAN: Of course they did. Why else would they split?

CLARE: You tell me.

BEVAN: I mean, God, they've lived separate lives for what, more than twenty-five years. That's a quarter of a century. Dad's a remarried man. They're probably up to their pewter anniversary or something. Alright, it's the frightful Fiona, but he seems to like her. He's cosily retired, living a life of ease.

CLARE: How would you know? You never see him.

BEVAN: He moved to Oz. He let it all go years ago. When are you going to?

CLARE, *shooting him a look*: I went up to Noosa to see him before he had his bypass. I thought somebody should. He told me these days it was as simple as changing the spark plugs on your car. But it's still heart surgery. People die.

BEVAN: I know.

CLARE: Of course I could hardly get twenty minutes with him away from Fiona. But I used to go on his walk with him – down to the beach every morning. It was only a couple of blocks but he'd have to shuffle along like an old man, he could barely keep his head up. One morning, sitting on the bench he always sat on, watching the surfers, he just started telling me how he took Mum out fishing once. Not long after they were married, she was pregnant with me. Dad said when it was time to come back the outboard wouldn't start. He figured he could swim for it – told Mum to sit tight for an hour. But the tide was running out really strongly and there was a cross-current. He said there were a couple of times he didn't think he'd make it. He came out way down the coast, had to climb up some cliffs. By the time he got back to the bach they were staying in, got the other dinghy in the water, it'd been four hours. It was dark. He had to row, shine the torch, row, shine the torch – looking for her. Calling out. Then when he saw the boat it was empty. He said he still has nightmares about it, thought he'd lost both of us. He rowed right up to it before Mum woke up. She was asleep in the bottom. Not worried in the slightest. He'd told her he'd be back. That was all she needed to know.

She looks at BEVAN.

And the look on his face, Bevan. He said, 'She'd have loved it here.'

BEVAN, *struggling*: Look – people come apart. It's happening every day. Some couples work, some don't.

CLARE: They loved each other.

BEVAN: They can't have at the end.

CLARE: Even at the end. Even after the end.

BEVAN: Clare – that's ridiculous. They broke up. Alright, Mum walked out. You don't do that if you still love each other.

CLARE: They did. And you know it. You're the only other person who can know it. And say it, Bevan.

BEVAN: I don't know it. I know what common sense tells me. And you have got to pull yourself out of this. (*He gets up and paces.*) Because it's pathetic, Clare. All this 'my parents broke up and robbed me of happiness'. You've got to move on. So OK, Gavin decided he wanted something else in his life. You've just got to – I don't know.

CLARE: Get over it?

BEVAN: Yes!

> *That was a bit too loud. They look at each other.*

I'm going to find the woman who runs this place. Get some milk or something. And ask her about Mum.

> CLARE *doesn't reply.* BEVAN *exits.* CLARE *sits there for a minute. She looks at the urn.*

CLARE: Now look what you've done. (*She lights a cigarette.*) Funny. Yesterday I was beside myself about you. Then this afternoon, driving down here, following your trail of breadcrumbs, I could feel myself getting so mad. It takes a bloody age to get out of Auckland. Have you ever noticed that? By the time I reached Ramarama I could have cheerfully killed you. If you weren't dead. And cremated. Then the rest of the way, I just got angrier and angrier and angrier. Let's just say it's probably lucky you came with Bevan. (*She flicks ash.*)

I don't know who I'm angry at. Gavin. You. Dad. Don't know why I'd be angry with Dad. Except that you left him. And that was that. He just got left. He didn't do anything about it, he didn't fight. He just let you go. (*She picks up the urn.*)

He didn't make you account for yourself. And now

who's going to? Eh? (*She gives it a shake.*) Eh?

BEVAN *comes back in.*

BEVAN: No answer at the house. There's nobody around. And I
mean nobody. (*He stops, seeing* CLARE *smoking and holding
the urn.*) You're not?
CLARE: I'm not.

She flicks ash on the floor, puts the urn back on the table.

But I am leaving. And I'm taking Mum with me. She's lain
in state for half an hour – that'll have to be enough.
BEVAN: She wanted to be here for the night.
CLARE: You're not going to find out what this place meant to
her. If anything. I'll take her back, drop her at the cemetery
tomorrow morning before I catch my plane.
BEVAN: I can do that.
CLARE: This way you don't have to go back to Auckland. You
can leave from here.
BEVAN: I don't mind.
CLARE: You've got a life to get on with in Wellington. You spent
enough time with Mum before she died.
BEVAN: Don't you want to find out if the owner knows her?
CLARE: Have you got a photo to show her?

BEVAN *looks blank.*

CLARE: What were you planning to do? (*She indicates the
urn.*) Hold this out and say, 'Have you seen this woman
before?'
BEVAN: She asked us to do this, Clare. It's the last thing.
CLARE: If I really believed it was the last thing – if I thought
I could walk out of here tomorrow morning with it all
squared away – then believe me, as grotesque as this place
is, I would do it. (CLARE *has finished her cigarette. She rises.*)
The light's going. I'm going to be driving in the dark.

BEVAN: Find a place round here. Come back in the morning.

CLARE: There is no place round here. I'm taking her, Bevan. This is one she doesn't get her own way. (*She rummages in her bag.*) Now I've really got to brush my teeth. (*She retrieves her toothbrush and looks towards the bathroom.*) If I dare.

> *She goes into the bathroom.* BEVAN *broods. There's a flash of light and a bang from off.*

CLARE, *off*: The bulb blew!

> BEVAN *picks up the urn decisively. He looks round, spots a high cupboard. He opens it (has to yank it because it's stuck) and puts the urn inside. It won't fit upright until he pulls out an encumbrance, a book –* Bitter Hill. *He glances at it, then takes more interest.*

BEVAN: The Thomas Case. (*He sees the date stamped in the back.*) Woah. That is seriously overdue.

CLARE, *off*: What?

BEVAN: Nothing.

> BEVAN *puts the book back in the cupboard and tries to shut the door. It won't go till he gives it a firm whack with the side of his fist. Suddenly there's a knocking and hammering of water pipes.*

CLARE, *off*: Jesus Christ!

BEVAN: What?

> CLARE *comes out horrified.*

CLARE: I turned on the tap and green slime came out.

BEVAN: What?

CLARE: Green slime. Out of the taps! (*She shudders.*) I had my toothbrush under it. I just dropped it. I can't even go back in there.

BEVAN: I'll get it.
CLARE: I don't want it!
BEVAN: Green slime?

> BEVAN *heads for the kitchen sink.*

CLARE: This place is beyond the pits. I just want to get out of here without touching another thing.

> BEVAN *turns the water on at the sink. The pipes again chug and bang, vomiting sporadic gushes of water.* CLARE *grabs her bag and looks round.*

Where's the urn? Bevan?

> BEVAN *is staring at the tap. He turns it on further.* CLARE *crosses to him.*

Bevan, where's Mum?
BEVAN: Water's a bit brown. But no –

> *The tap erupts, spitting and gagging something long and viscous into the sink.* BEVAN *recoils but* CLARE *leaps back.*

CLARE: Oh! Oh my God! I'm going to be sick!

> BEVAN *steps towards the sink. He squints at the contents of the sink and what's still trailing from the tap. He looks round for an implement, yanks open a stuck drawer and takes out a tarnished fork.*

Bevan.

> BEVAN *hooks a slimy strand and lifts it up to examine it better in the grey light coming through the window.*

BEVAN: It's not slime. It's some kind of plant.
CLARE: A plant?
BEVAN: Growing in the water pipes.

BEVAN *reaches to shut the tap off but it's stuck.*

Now it won't turn off.

The pipes continue to hammer, and water continues to spurt into the sink.

CLARE: This is for the Health Department. How they can expect people to stay here—
BEVAN: If people do stay here.

CLARE *looks at him.*

In this unit at least. I had a look through some of the other windows. They've all been done up. Modernised. The decor's completely different to this one.

BEVAN *starts opening cupboards – looking. He finds a jiffy iron, a plumber's plunger . . .*

CLARE: Bevan, this place is seriously giving me the creeps. I want to get out of here right now. And I want you to come with me. And Mum. (*He glances round.*) Where is she?
BEVAN: Look. Here's your curtains.

BEVAN *pulls a folded curtain from where* MRS WICKS *has stuffed it in a cupboard, and throws it open in a shower of dust and desiccated fibres.*

Rotted.

He climbs on a chair to hold the curtain up to the window so the bleached, rotted, rent square matches the window frame – darker, un-sun-destroyed fabric framing it where the curtain has extended below the window and to one side of it.

CLARE: Enough, Bevan. Let's just get Mum and get out of here.

CLARE crosses to Bevan's bag and looks in it for the urn.

BEVAN: Another thing.

BEVAN drops the curtain and moves to the indentations he noticed earlier in the carpet.

See? (*He gets down on the floor and taps one.*) The carpet's been compressed so long it's like fibreglass. She moved that chair. (*He moves towards the chair but winces as something jabs into his knee.*) Ow.

BEVAN picks something up from the carpet.

CLARE: What is it?
BEVAN: A bullet.
CLARE: A live bullet?
BEVAN: A spent one.

CLARE takes a step closer to look.

CLARE: That's neither. It's a cartridge case.
BEVAN: Daddy's girl.

He stands, places the cartridge case on the benchtop. He looks towards the chair.

CLARE: Bevan, stop mucking around.

BEVAN crosses to the chair –

Bevan, I'm freaked out enough!

– and lifts it intending to place it back where its legs fit the hollows in the carpet. He stops. They both stare at the large discoloured stain revealed where the chair was sitting.

It's not.
BEVAN: How do you know?
CLARE: It's just not.

BEVAN: Blood would go that colour. I think. Something like that.

CLARE: You don't know.

> BEVAN *squats to examine the stain, squinting in the dim light from the single bulb.*

BEVAN: Hard to tell. Could be rainwater leaking in – picking up rust from the roof.

CLARE: There you go then.

BEVAN, *looking up*: Except there's no stain on the ceiling. Switch that lamp on.

> CLARE *leans over to switch on the lamp on the small table. There's a blue sparking flash and a minor explosion behind the table as the wiring blows up.* CLARE *springs back with a scream. Simultaneously a fuse blows and the one working light snaps off.*
>
> *Smoke rises from behind the table.* BEVAN *looks cautiously behind. He reaches down and flicks the wall switch off. He reaches for the lamp.*

CLARE: Don't touch it!

BEVAN: It's alright. (*He picks up the lamp. The trailing cord ends abruptly.*) The cord shorted right through. (*He rubs a section of cord in his fingers, turning it to dust.*) The insulation's just crumbling away.

CLARE: I'm going to phone the police. (*She gets her phone out of her bag then hesitates.*) What's their number?

BEVAN: Their number?

CLARE: I can't call 111 – that's an emergency line. There's a fine for misusing it. They'll ask what the nature of the emergency is.

BEVAN: Well – the lights've gone out. The tap won't turn off. And there's a stain.

CLARE: You're not helping, Bevan!

BEVAN: Stop panicking. OK, we'll go. But first let's see if we can get to the bottom of this.

He looks around.

CLARE: I've got a better idea. Let's not.

BEVAN: There was something else she got rid of in a hurry. On the table.

He finds the scrunched-up newspaper MRS WICKS *dropped in the kitchen bin. As he unwraps it, something leathery and unpleasant falls out on the floor.*

CLARE, *recoiling*: Ugh! What is it?

BEVAN, *picking it up by the tail*: Looks like a flounder. Fossilised.

BEVAN *glances at a page of the newspaper then stops dead, staring. He zeroes in on the date at the top of the page.*

No.

CLARE *looks over his shoulder and is horrified.*

CLARE: Oh my God. Oh my God.

They stare at each other.

Now are you coming?

BEVAN'*s gaze has returned to the newspaper.*

BEVAN: She didn't want us in here.

CLARE: Bevan, that's thirty years old!

BEVAN: 1973. (*He puts it down.*) What do we do if we see her?

CLARE: We're popping out for dinner, that's all. Is there anyone else besides her?

BEVAN: I don't think so. There was a son.

CLARE: Was?

BEVAN: He's – 'not here any more'.

CLARE: What?

BEVAN: There was something weird about the way she said that.

CLARE: Is the coast clear?

> BEVAN *looks.*

BEVAN: Can't see anyone.

CLARE: Put the chair back.

BEVAN: What?

CLARE: So no one knows we've seen.

> BEVAN *shifts the chair back to its original position.*

OK. (*She takes a breath.*) Just popping out for dinner.

BEVAN: With my bag. (*He grabs it.*)

CLARE: Hold it to your side so it's not so obvious.

BEVAN: Get your keys out. (*She looks at him.*) You've got me blocked in with that cafe tractor you rented. If things turn parochial I don't want to be stuck there while you fossick around in your handbag.

CLARE, *fossicking*: I don't have to fossick. They're right . . . Have you got Mum? That's the main thing.

BEVAN: Mum.

> *He goes to the cupboard and tugs on the door. It's jammed.*
> CLARE *doesn't notice, intensifying her slightly panicked search for her keys in her bag.*

CLARE: I put them right – (*Bevan pulls again, harder.*) – here!

> *As* CLARE *produces the keys triumphantly,* BEVAN *heaves on the cupboard door. The cupboard handle snaps off in his hand.*

BEVAN: Shit.
CLARE: What?
BEVAN: Shit.

> *He tries to pull on the stubs of the handle but can't get a grip.*

CLARE: She's not in there?
BEVAN: In here? No, no, no – she's not in here.

> *He whacks the cupboard.*

CLARE: What did you put her in there for?
BEVAN: Does that actually matter now?
CLARE: I think I'd like to know!
BEVAN: To stop you pulling your Gestapo routine!
CLARE: What?
BEVAN: She wanted to be here for the night.
CLARE: Well she must be laughing now! Are you getting anywhere?

> BEVAN *is struggling with the cupboard.*

BEVAN: It's jammed.
CLARE: I can see that!

> BEVAN *heads for the kitchen drawer looking for an implement to prise with.*

BEVAN: Just like Dad.
CLARE: What?
BEVAN: You! You're so rigid. You said it yourself – Constable Clare. You can't tolerate life's uncertainties or loose ends. Everything's got to be instantly classifiable – so you can tidy it all up, tidy it away.
CLARE: Don't talk to me about tidying. That must be the first thing you've put away in your life!

BEVAN, *prising*: All that 'a place for everything and everything in its place'.

CLARE: Someone has to organise things. We can't all be flaky!

BEVAN: Flaky?

CLARE: I'm sorry. You're obviously in complete command of the situation!

BEVAN: And you can't figure out why Gavin left you! How about how you have to control everything?

CLARE: Just shut up, Bevan! Just shut up – and get Mum out of there!

> *A silhouette has appeared at the kitchen window – and now ducks away unseen as* CLARE *turns, very upset. She slumps into a chair.* BEVAN *knows he's gone too far. The bread-and-butter knife he's prising with bends.*

BEVAN: Shit.

CLARE, *distraught*: A place for everything.

BEVAN, *prising*: That's why I could never have been a cop.

CLARE: Everything in its place. Like the garage.

BEVAN, *stopping*: I'm getting nowhere here, Clare.

CLARE: Dad's garage.

BEVAN: Eh?

CLARE: How all the tools had that painted silhouette so you knew where to hang them back up. Everything in its place.

BEVAN: Are you OK?

CLARE: That's why Gavin left me. I said he should do that.

BEVAN: What?

CLARE: In the garage. The tools were everywhere.

BEVAN: You suggested he paint little silhouettes? And he left? It can't have been just because of that.

CLARE: I don't know why I said it. I think because I knew what he'd do.

BEVAN: It's never just one thing. It's a hundred things.

CLARE: I bought the paint.

BEVAN: That's just the last thing that happened. That doesn't tell you anything.

CLARE: And if I knew the first thing? Would that tell me?

BEVAN: I don't know, Clare.

CLARE: Was the first thing Mum and Dad? Was it?

BEVAN: I don't know.

CLARE: What hope did we have? If they couldn't stay together when they loved each other, what hope did that leave us?

BEVAN: I don't know, I don't have the answer!

> *He turns away. Pause.*

I was with Mum in the supermarket once when we ran into Dad. I thought Mum was going to fall down. There's nothing like watching your parents crying into their separate tins of baked beans to screw a kid up.

You want to know what hope I had? I had plenty. Stupid kid-stuff hope that they might get back together. Even with Dad marrying the frightful Fiona. I managed to cling onto the idea that they might still magically fall into place again the same way they fell apart. I couldn't seem to give it up.

CLARE: Until when?

BEVAN, *looking round, tears in his eyes*: I guess I can stop holding my breath for that now.

> CLARE *goes to him and puts her arms around him. They hold each other.*

I'm sorry about the Christmas cards.

CLARE: The what?

BEVAN: Your Christmas cards. I like to know what you're doing.

> CLARE *laughs and takes a breath. With a jolt of pipes the water running into the sink abruptly stops.* BEVAN *and*

CLARE *stare at the tap in the sudden silence.*

They've shut the water off.

They look at each other.

CLARE: Let's just get out of here.

BEVAN *glances at the recalcitrant cupboard.*

BEVAN: We'll have to leave her here.
CLARE: Leave her?
BEVAN: For now. There's no point the whole family ending up in the cupboard. Or somewhere worse.
CLARE: If we're going, we're going together. All of us.

She rummages round in the kitchen.

BEVAN: At least Mum died of natural causes. That's starting to look quite attractive.

CLARE *comes up with the plunger.*

Perished.

CLARE *chooses to ignore this. With do-or-die determination she charges the cupboard and whacks the plunger onto it. The suction holds. She yanks on the plunger and with a graunch the cupboard door flies open.*

Way to go!

CLARE *pulls the urn out of the cupboard (the book also tumbling out onto the floor) and cradles it protectively.* BEVAN *picks up both his and Clare's bags.*

CLARE: Right.

They head for the door. BEVAN *opens it.* MRS WICKS *is standing there with a hatchet. They recoil.*

Mrs Wicks: I've brought a candle.

They just stare at her.

You must have blown a fuse.

Bevan, *eyeing the hatchet*: You normally fix a fuse with that?

Mrs Wicks: I saw you having trouble with the cupboard. I thought if the worst came to the worst we could . . . (*She makes a chopping motion.*)

They stare at her. She steps inside. They step back. She's blocking their exit.

This has all gone a bit wrong. You shouldn't be here.

Bevan: Actually, we're just on our way.

Clare: Out for dinner.

Mrs Wicks: You're meant to be up at the house. With me.

Bevan: Thanks, but we've really got to get going.

Mrs Wicks: It's all the wrong way round. I wanted to explain. At the house. Then bring you here.

Clare: Explain?

Mrs Wicks: But I panicked. When I saw you. I thought it was tomorrow. I'm sure you said tomorrow on the phone. The ninth.

Bevan, *as Clare shoots him a glance*: It's possible.

Mrs Wicks: When you were suddenly here . . . and when I saw you, Clare.

Clare: How do you know my name?

Bevan, *asserting himself*: Look, this is obviously not what any of us had in mind, so let's forget the whole thing.

Mrs Wicks: You can't leave.

Bevan: Yes we can. And that's what we're going to do. So if you'll just – bury the hatchet.

Mrs Wicks: What?

Bevan: Put that down.

Mrs Wicks looks at the hatchet. She lays it on the bench.

Mrs Wicks: What did you think I was going to do?
Bevan: Clare.

He ushers her towards the door.

Mrs Wicks, *to* Clare: You're so much like her, you see.

Clare *stops, staring at her.*

Mrs Wicks: Like Jan.
Bevan: You knew Mum.

She looks at the urn Clare *is holding.*

Mrs Wicks: I suppose – that's her?
Clare: Who are you?
Mrs Wicks: Just a friend. She'd come and stay with me.
Clare: Here?
Mrs Wicks: No. In the house. Once here.
Bevan: Thirty years ago? 1973?
Clare: No one's been in here – since Mum was here?
Mrs Wicks: I took the number off the door and just left it. No one noticed.
Bevan: It's been closed up all this time?
Mrs Wicks: Until this afternoon.
Bevan: Why?
Mrs Wicks: I knew Jan was coming. I'd been putting it off.
Bevan: No – why keep it like this?
Mrs Wicks: Your father told me not to touch anything.
Clare: Dad?
Mrs Wicks: I think he meant in the short term. But I suppose the more time went past, the easier it was to ignore. Jan always said I had to face it one day. This is her idea of giving me a push. May I?

She gestures towards the urn. CLARE *and* BEVAN *look at each other.*

She's come all this way.

CLARE hesitates, then holds the urn out. MRS WICKS *takes it and cradles it.*

BEVAN: Those are her shoes, aren't they?
MRS WICKS: She passed a lot of things on.

She places the urn carefully on the table and sits in front of it.

We'll get her set up here. Then go up to the house where it's warm. I've got the fire on. We can have a cup of something while we talk.

MRS WICKS takes a CD player out of the bag she's carrying.

BEVAN: What's that?
MRS WICKS: Her music.

She arranges it beside the urn. She takes a candle holder with a single candle out of her bag and places it on the other side of the urn.

She had a talent for being happy. Don't you think?

This has never occurred to CLARE.

CLARE: I suppose she did.
MRS WICKS: The last time we were in this room I told her I was alright by myself. She knew that wasn't the truth. She came back. Then I had someone I could talk to – and everything changed. (*She looks at them.*) You see, I'm the same as you. It's because of her I'm here.

Mrs Wicks gestures beside her.

Will you light the candle, Clare?

Clare sits, takes the matches Mrs Wicks offers and lights the candle.

And Bevan?
Bevan: Sorry?

She indicates the other side. Bevan sits.

Mrs Wicks: Push play.

Bevan sets the CD playing. It is 'Dirty Work' by Steely Dan. They look at the tableau. Music ('Dirty Work') up as the rest of the lights slowly fade, leaving only the candle glowing.

Light

*1973. February. The Midway Motel – Unit Five. As before,
but thirty years younger: the curtains hang in the windows, the
armchair is in its original position. There's no stain on the carpet.
The picture hangs straight. There is the sound of birds outside. It
is a warm summer's evening. A chunky cassette player of the era
is on the table. It's playing Steely Dan's 'Dirty Work'.* JAN – 34,
*with a quick, darting intelligence – is arranging an armchair
carefully, consulting a page of a book,* Bitter Hill *(which she's
bookmarked with a postcard). She positions her shoes in front of
the armchair then props a mop and a bucket up on the chair, the
bucket approximating someone's head if they were sitting in the
chair. Checking the orientation of everything,* JAN *opens the louvre
windows and goes out.*

A moment later PHILLIP *– an awkward young man – knocks quietly
on the open door (which has the number five on it).*

PHILLIP: Hello?

> PHILLIP *enters, carrying fresh towels. Laying the towels
> down he notices the strange arrangement of armchair,
> mop and bucket. Puzzled, he hoists the mop, intending
> to tidy the things away, but notices the shoes on the floor.
> He glances round, then slips his foot into one of Jan's shoes.
> He glances round again then sits in the chair and bends
> down to pull the ankle strap of the shoe up (still holding the
> mop and bucket).* JAN *appears (balanced on something)
> outside the louvre windows holding a long-handled
> plumber's plunger which she is using to approximate a
> rifle. Struggling with her awkward position, she carefully
> points the 'rifle' through the open louvres, squinting down
> it as she attempts to sight on the bucket – which wobbles
> slightly as the unseen* PHILLIP *works the strap up over his*

heel. Just as JAN *is satisfied with her aim and goes to 'fire',* PHILLIP, *shoe firmly on, sits up.*

JAN: Bang!

> PHILLIP *springs to his feet, knocking over the mop and bucket.*

Oh, sorry!

> JAN *disappears from the window.* PHILLIP, *panicked, quickly kicks off the shoe and starts for the door, but* JAN *comes in it.*

It's not loaded.

> *She waves the plunger at him. She turns off the cassette player.*

I didn't think anyone was here.

PHILLIP, *picking them up*: I brought new towels.

JAN: Oh.

PHILLIP: I should get the old ones.

JAN: I will.

> JAN *vanishes into the bathroom.* PHILLIP *lays the towels down again, and starts to carefully fold and arrange them.* JAN *comes back with the damp towels. She watches him.*

You scallop them.

> PHILLIP *is folding the towels so they fan out from a square fold.*

Did your mother show you that?

> PHILLIP *shakes his head. He finishes. They admire the result.* JAN *holds out the plunger.*

I got it from the laundry. And the other things. Sorry, I was going to put them all back.

Phillip takes the plunger. Joking, he works an imaginary bolt to unload it. Jan smiles. Phillip hovers a moment.

PHILLIP: I saw towels like that in McKenzies. In boxes.

JAN: Those look like they should be in boxes.

PHILLIP: I taught myself. I'm probably the only person for five miles round who knows how to do that.

JAN: Are there many people for five miles round?

PHILLIP, *hesitating*: Not really. No.

JAN: It does seem a bit . . . isolated.

PHILLIP: I wouldn't really know. I've lived here all my life.

JAN: What's it midway between?

PHILLIP: Sorry?

JAN: Why's it called the Midway Motel?

PHILLIP: It was a choice between that and the Mountain View Motel.

JAN: But there isn't a mountain.

PHILLIP: There is. You just can't see it from here. It's sort of a trick of the light. You'd be amazed how close we are. People are always amazed.

JAN: That they can't see it?

PHILLIP: Well, one person was. But he was really amazed. And I could see his point.

JAN: You just can't see the mountain's point.

PHILLIP: No, that's right. (*Realising it's a joke.*) That's funny.

JAN: But you didn't call it the Mountain View.

PHILLIP: No.

JAN: You chose Midway.

PHILLIP: Mum did. It fitted on the sign better.

JAN: So it's not really midway between anything?

PHILLIP: Midway between bankruptcy and our first million – according to Mum.

JAN: Oh. Must be a slow day today.

> PHILLIP *looks baffled.*

I noticed it only seems to be us here. We're the only occupied unit.

PHILLIP: It's not really the season.

JAN: When is the season?

PHILLIP: Are you in the motel business?

JAN: No.

PHILLIP: I suppose – summer.

JAN: Christmas. People coming on holiday.

PHILLIP: Well, you wouldn't really come on holiday here.

JAN: You get more people coming through for work reasons?

PHILLIP: Not a lot of work any more.

JAN: There used to be more work?

PHILLIP, *uncomfortable*: Probably . . . about the same.

JAN: Oh.

> *Pause.*

PHILLIP: Is your husband looking for work?

JAN: Tom? He doesn't need any more work.

PHILLIP: I thought that might be why you were asking.

JAN: I'd never see him.

PHILLIP: I thought you might be thinking of opening a motel.

JAN: Tom and I running a motel? I suppose it is an idea. For when Tom retires, I mean. Especially since you're doing so well.

> PHILLIP *looks puzzled.*

Since you've made half a million dollars.

PHILLIP, *slightly alarmed*: We haven't made half a million dollars. Who said we had half a million dollars?

JAN: You did. I mean, your mother did. That you were halfway to a million dollars.

PHILLIP: No, that's just Mum's joke.
JAN: Right.
PHILLIP: Half a million dollars!
JAN: It did seem a lot.
PHILLIP: You'd have to be a millionaire to have that kind of
money.

Pause.

Do you want the *Herald* again in the morning?
JAN: Please.

He collects the mop and bucket. JAN *picks up the book.*
PHILLIP *heads for the door.* JAN's *reminded of something
by the book.*

Have you got a gun?
PHILLIP: Sorry?
JAN: Sorry – what's your name?
PHILLIP: Phillip.
JAN: Phillip. I was just wondering if you had a gun I could use?

PHILLIP *just looks at her.*

Everyone's got one out here, haven't they?
PHILLIP: You don't need a gun here. This is the country.
JAN: Oh. So you've never owned a rifle? (*She glances at the open
page of the book.*) A point two-two?
PHILLIP: Me?
JAN: Yes.
PHILLIP: No.
JAN: Oh.
PHILLIP: Can I have the towels please?

JAN *picks up the armload of damp towels and hands them
to him. He puts the plunger down to balance the other
things.*

JAN: It's just I thought you must know about guns when you
did that with the plunger. You know – (*she imitates his
unloading action*) – when you did that, pulling back on the
– whatever it is –
PHILLIP: Bolt.
JAN: – on the bolt.

> *They both realise what he's just said.*

I thought you said you'd never had one.
PHILLIP: I didn't.
JAN: What?
PHILLIP: Say that.
JAN: I thought you did.
PHILLIP, *feeling cornered*: You said 'owned' and that's what I
answered and I was telling the truth so it's no use trying
to trip me up!

> *Pause.*

Sorry.
JAN: I've upset you.
PHILLIP: No.
JAN: Yes, I have.
PHILLIP: You're our guest.
JAN: Does that mean I'm allowed to upset you? Sorry. Too many
questions. Would you like a cup of tea? Oh no. That's
another one.

> *They look at each other and laugh.*

PHILLIP: I've got the towels to do. And your husband will be
back soon.
JAN: I'm not so sure. He's working.
PHILLIP: Round here?
JAN: I can't tell you what he's doing. I'm not supposed to know
myself.

PHILLIP: Sounds like a secret agent.

JAN: No, he's more like . . . Superman, coming to the rescue.

PHILLIP: So you don't want to shoot him then?

> *It is* JAN'*s turn to look puzzled.* PHILLIP *indicates the chair, the louvres, and sights an imaginary rifle.*

JAN: Oh! No, of course not! Poor old Tom. He's not that late. I was asking about the gun because I thought, if you happened to have a point two-two, I could do a little test with it.

PHILLIP: Test?

JAN: A little one. To see how far the thingy springs.

> PHILLIP *looks at her blankly.*

> When you do that – (*she imitates him working the bolt*) – after firing – and the little thingy springs out.

PHILLIP: Cartridge case.

JAN: That's it. I wanted to see how far it –

PHILLIP: Springs. (PHILLIP *looks at her a moment.*) You need a licence.

JAN: Sorry?

PHILLIP: You get in trouble if you have a gun and no licence.

JAN: I don't have a licence.

PHILLIP: Neither have I. It's not mine. It's my mother's twenty-two.

JAN: I haven't actually seen your mother.

PHILLIP: She's . . . not here right now.

JAN: Oh.

PHILLIP: Did you say yes to the *Herald*?

JAN: Yes.

> *Juggling the mop, bucket and towels,* PHILLIP *exits.* JAN *notices the plunger on the floor and picks it up.*

Oh – you've forgotten the . . .

But he's gone. JAN *looks round, picks up the book and flips a few pages. She sits at the table reading, face propped on her hand. She starts to feel her face, nursing it as if it's injured – jaw or nose broken. She starts to moan as if wracked with throbbing pain. She gets up and staggers about, her face in her hand. She collapses to her knees, sobbing. She fumbles for the phone blindly and (without dialling) speaks into it.*

JAN, *sobbing, at the end of her tether*: I can't. I can't take it any more. No, Dad, it's too late.

She puts the phone down and picks up the plunger. Slumping into the chair, she holds the 'muzzle' of her imaginary rifle against her temple. She stretches out her leg and fishes with her big toe to find the 'trigger'. It takes a few attempts but, having got it, she bites her lip and jerks her toe. She flings herself sideways in the chair under the impact of the imagined bullet.

Pause. JAN *sits up, fully recovered and pleased with her charade.*

Hmm. (*There is the sound of whistling outside.* JAN *jumps up, and is seized with cramp in her trigger toe.*)
   Ooh. Ow!

She quickly hobbles to the kitchen to shove the plunger into a cupboard. Spotting the book on the table, she hops desperately over to grab it, looking for somewhere to hide it. With no time to do anything else, she thrusts it under the seat cushion of the armchair, just as TOM *comes in.*

TOM: Sorry I'm late, hon. But – I brought dinner.

He flourishes a parcel of fish and chips, which he lays on the table. Even in his civvies TOM *exudes a bluff solidity which*

says cop: able, affable, reliable and – at 36 – poised to go
all the way in the police élite. He comes across and kisses
JAN. *She grimaces.*

What's the matter?
JAN: Cramp. In my big toe.
TOM: Oh, baby.

He picks up her foot and starts to massage her toe.

JAN: Ooh. Ow. Ooh.

She topples backwards into the armchair and TOM *kneels*
in front of her, rubbing and bending her toe.

TOM: Gotcha. All to myself. All tomorrow. All tonight, come to
think of it. (*He nibbles her toe. She shrieks and struggles. He*
holds her foot and bites.) It's good for cramp.

Laughing, JAN *manages to twist her foot free.*

All cured?
JAN: Now I've got stitch.

TOM *buries his face in her side, giving it the same treatment.*
JAN *wriggles as he works his way up to kiss her. Slowly this*
time.

You've been drinking.
TOM: One or two. Nothing over the odds.
JAN: Where?
TOM: Some pub. Like something out of the thirties. (*He gets up.*)
But – with a great fish and chip shop right next door. (*He*
crosses to the table to unwrap the fish and chips, but shuts the
parcel as JAN *crosses.*) Guess.
JAN: Fish and chips? (TOM *raises an eyebrow.*) Oh Tom, not
potato fritters? (*Apparently not.*) Rissoles?

TOM: I'll give you rissoles. (*He opens the parcel with a flourish.*) Flounder.

JAN, *giving him the reaction he's after*: No!

TOM: Too bloody right two beautiful flounder! When was the last time you saw that in our local?

JAN, *spotting a third flounder*: Who's the other one for?

TOM: Must've chucked an extra in for free. Country hospitality.

JAN: I bet they knew you were police.

TOM: I didn't tell them.

JAN: Who were you drinking with?

TOM, *eating chips*: Couple of the boys from Auckland Central.

JAN: Did they come down to help you?

TOM: You could say that. Rustle up some plates, hon. It'll get cold.

> JAN *goes to the kitchenette and finds plates in a cupboard.*

JAN: Uniform?

TOM: No, couple of Ds. I went through the college with one of them. Haven't seen him for years. Oh, and the local PC popped in. And forgot to pop out again.

> JAN *brings the plates and* TOM *starts to pile handfuls of chips onto them.*

JAN: You haven't washed your hands.

TOM: I haven't been touching anything.

JAN: My toe.

TOM: Don't tell me you haven't washed your toe before coming to the table? (*He slides a flounder onto each plate.*) There you go. Fit for a king. And his wife. (*He starts eating.*) Look at that. Just falls apart.

> JAN *toys with hers.*

JAN: Must have been important. (*He looks at her, mouth full.*)
   What you were doing today.
TOM: Just an excuse to get you and me away on a break.
JAN: Did you tell anyone at work you were bringing me?
TOM, *grinning*: First rule at HQ: What they don't know doesn't
   hurt them. There any sauce?
JAN: In the kitchen.

   As TOM *heads to the kitchen and opens a cupboard,*
   looking –

TOM: I remember flounder for breakfast. Dredging them up in a
   net off the beach when I was staying at my grandad's. First
   thing in the morning up and out. Watching the sun come
   up over the sea. (*He comes up with the plunger and looks at*
   it.) That fills you with confidence.
JAN: Try looking with your woman's eyes.
TOM: Eh?
JAN: In the box!

   TOM *spots the box on the bench containing supplies they've*
   brought with them, and takes out a bottle of tomato
   sauce.

TOM, *sitting down again*: Seeing what it's like out here makes me
   wonder if our two are missing out.
JAN: On what?
TOM, *shrugging*: Outdoorsy stuff. Getting your hands wet, getting
   dirty, but coming home with something. Small towns and
   sea. Say what you like, that's what this country is.
JAN: Oh yes? Planning to move us all out into the wop-wops
   now?
TOM, *eating*: No worries there. It's Wellington for us from here
   on in. HQ all the way.
JAN: No more transfers.
TOM: No more transfers. No more upping sticks every two years.

The kids can settle into their schools. The Commissioner likes me, Jan. I reckon he's lining me up for big things.

JAN: It's only what you deserve.

TOM: Course I bloody deserve it! So do you! (*He leans across the table, a chip romantically wedged in his teeth. They nibble their way into a kiss.*) Ever fancied going to Fiji?

JAN: Fiji?

TOM: You, me and the kids – a proper holiday. White sand beaches, coconut palms.

JAN: Policemen in skirts.

TOM: Not exactly girls' blouses though. Played them at rugby once. (*He winces.*)

JAN: Bevan and Clare would love it. Swimming all day, exploring . . . Bevan needs to spend more time with you.

TOM: Why especially Bevan?

JAN: Both of them.

TOM: Clare's had to put up with not seeing me just as much.

JAN: She doesn't seem to need to see you. She just adores you.

TOM: What d'you mean – Bevan doesn't?

JAN: No, of course not. A boy likes to do things with his father, that's all.

TOM: Could've fooled me.

JAN: He does.

TOM: He's getting too old to be traipsing along with me anyway.

JAN: Tom, he's only eight.

TOM: I just don't – I can't seem to teach him anything. He's too busy asking questions. Why this? Why that? Why not this way?

JAN: That's how children learn.

TOM: Yeah, well another way to learn is to shut this, keep these open and accept what you're being told once in a while.

JAN *looks down at her flounder.*

I blame new maths. They bring that home. You can't make head or tail of it. They decide you don't know a bloody thing. (TOM *puts his slight irritation behind him. He looks around.*) I'm sorry, Jan. (*She looks at him.*) Leaving you here all day. It's a bloody dead and alive hole. I'll give the Commissioner's secretary a wind-up when I get back. Booking me in here. Suppose it was the only place handy.

JAN: I don't mind. If it's all in a good cause.

    JAN *seems about to ask something.*

TOM: Seen the joker who runs it?

JAN: He came to change the towels.

TOM: Something weird about him. Shifty.

JAN: I think it's nice the way he's helping out his mother.

TOM: His mother? You must've got the wrong end of the stick there, Jan.

JAN: Why?

TOM: That local cop at the pub was telling me. Reckons they hardly ever see him. Real mummy's boy he said – up until she died a year or so ago.

    JAN *takes this in.*

JAN: Poor boy.

    TOM *moves across to her.*

TOM: First thing in the morning we're out of here. Lunch in Queen Street – a bit of shopping.

JAN: Remind me to send Clare her postcard.

TOM: We'll be back before it arrives.

JAN: They love getting mail. I hope they're not fighting.

TOM: They'll be fine with Mum and Dad. Relax. Now the business is out of the way, time for some pleasure. (*He strokes her hand.*) Can't remember the last time we had a couple of days to ourselves.

He dances with her. They're close.

JAN: What was it about? Today.

TOM: Eh?

JAN: Where did you go?

TOM: Come on, Jan, that's work.

JAN: We've come all this way. It must be important.

TOM: You're the one who said you didn't want to know about work.

JAN: Years ago. When you were on the beat or in the cars. The more I knew the more I worried.

TOM: Yeah, well, no need to worry any more. We're home and hosed.

JAN: That's what I mean. This is different, isn't it? It's not like when you'd come home with stories about drunks and accidents and stabbings and there was nothing I could do. With this, you can talk to me, and I can help.

TOM: Help?

JAN: Because I'm right outside of it.

TOM, *tapping her forehead*: What's got in under that bonnet, eh? What's going on in there?

JAN: I know where we are, Tom. And what happened here. It's in the paper every other day. All about the new trial.

TOM: Honey . . . (*He takes her hands.*) Yeah, this is a big one. There's a lot riding on it. There's a special job the Commissioner wants done. So he asked me to take a look at it. He asked me, Jan. What d'you think that says?

JAN: That he'd better look out for his job.

TOM: Eh?

JAN: Because you'll be Commissioner before long.

TOM, *laughing*: It's about twenty years too soon for that. Police commissioners are like popes – you've got to wait for them to fall off the perch.

(*Serious.*) Thing is, if we don't get this right we'll all be looking to our jobs. That's why he wants it low-key. I report back to him and him only.

JAN: He trusts you to tell him. I knew it! I knew that's what you were doing. Where did you go today? To the house?

TOM: Hold on, Jan. I've just told you it's secret squirrel.

JAN: That doesn't include your wife. Does it?

> TOM *looks at her, amused by her pent-up excitement and enjoying being the man in the know.*

Just tell me one thing, Tom. One thing. (TOM *looks at her.*) You went to the house today, didn't you? Where it happened.

> TOM *relents.*

TOM, *nodding*: Yeah.

JAN: What was it like?

TOM, *shrugging*: A house. Lawn needs mowing. Whole place is a bit untidy.

JAN: Untidy?

TOM: Washing everywhere. Kids' toys.

JAN: Still?

TOM: No, from the family there now.

JAN: There's people living there? In the house?

TOM: Young couple. Pretty used to the attention by the look of it. I guess they get sightseers as well as our lot. Certainly didn't go to any special trouble.

JAN: How could they do it?

TOM: Must've got it cheap.

JAN: I couldn't. I wouldn't.

TOM: You can't pull down a house every time there's a murder. Plenty of people living right on top of things they don't know about. (*He looks round.*) We've got no way of knowing what's happened in here before. And you slept OK last night. (*He advances on her with a* Psycho-*themed, stabbing motion.*)

JAN: Tom!

TOM: Cup of tea? (*He crosses to fill the jug.*)

JAN: Were there any curtains?

TOM: Eh?

JAN: Did they have curtains up?

TOM: I didn't notice.

JAN: How could you not notice?

TOM: I wasn't there to look at curtains.

JAN: Who did you talk to?

TOM: I told you. The boys from Auckland.

JAN: No, I mean who else? Did you talk to the boy who saw the woman? At the house. The woman who was standing at the gate two days after it must have happened.

> TOM *is looking at her.*

TOM: Where're you getting all this from?

JAN, *eager*: Because if that boy saw her, and he can say what she looked like, then that changes everything, doesn't it?

TOM: Steady on, Jan. You don't want to get carried away with what you read in the papers.

JAN: So you didn't talk to him?

TOM: No.

JAN: I thought he'd be your best witness.

TOM: That's not up to me. I'm not coming in telling anyone how to do their police work. These jokers have been in the job for years.

JAN: If you'd been in charge from the beginning there wouldn't need to be a new trial.

TOM: I'm not saying you're wrong there.

JAN: That's why the Commissioner's sent you, because he knows you'll get to the bottom of it.

TOM, *grinning*: The way he put it, it's all about keeping our bottom out of it. (*He reacts to* JAN's *puzzled look.*) Making sure it's not a down-trou in court. That we're not left standing there, uniform daks round our ankles, the bare arse of law enforcement in this country out there for all to see. Balls blowing in the wind.

JAN: If it looks like there's been a mistake.

TOM: Exactly. That idea starts to get bandied round, next minute it's why can't the whole New Zealand Police Force be a cock-up from start to finish?

JAN: That's silly.

TOM: Of course it's silly. But that's the way some people out there are starting to think. If they're not saying we've got our heads stuck in the ground over this, it's that we've done some sort of job on poor old Mr Thomas.

JAN: One mistake doesn't mean the police are bad or wrong. All you have to do is correct the mistake and people will see that.

TOM, *looking at* JAN: You haven't been listening to any of that, have you? That the cops on the inquiry framed him and now we're all trying to cover it up?

JAN: Of course not.

TOM: Good. (*He turns away.*)

JAN: I just think they got it wrong.

TOM *stops. He turns back.*

TOM: Wrong?

JAN, *nodding*: Mmm.

TOM: You do? You think that?

JAN, *nodding again*: Mmm.

TOM: You ever been at a crime scene, Jan?

JAN: You know I haven't.

TOM: You've never lifted a fingerprint, ruled out a grid search? Never stared at a witness or a suspect trying to figure out if they're giving you something roughly approximating the truth or just 100 per cent pure bullshit.

JAN: No, but you have. And that's why I thought— [*you'd talk to him.*]

Tom: Then why don't you leave it to the experts, eh?

Jan: I can have an opinion.

Tom: No you can't.

Jan: I can.

Tom: You can't have your own opinion about something you know next to nothing about. You could have my opinion. Or the opinion of someone else who's gotten in your ear. But if you've never even seen the place, read the file, talked to the people concerned, how can you formulate any idea about what actually happened?

Jan: That's what I'm saying.

Tom: Eh?

Jan: You haven't either. Talked to the people concerned. You haven't talked to that boy who saw the woman at the gate.

Tom: Who claims to have seen her! To have seen someone. Who could have got the wrong day, the wrong week, whose eyesight could be shot and his imagination out of control, who could just be saying it for the hell of it, to get some attention, who could've been looking at a bloke in a dress for all he knows!

Jan: But how can you know without talking to him? I'm just wondering how you've formulated your opinion?

Tom *looks at her.*

Tom: Who says I've got an opinion?

Jan: Tom.

Tom: I'm here to investigate. First thing with that is keep an open mind. You've got to keep the personal out of it.

Jan: But you've finished.

Tom: I haven't written my report yet.

Jan: You know what it's going to say.

Tom: How do I know, Jan?

Jan: I know you, Tom. You've made up your mind.

TOM: I've got to let things settle. I've only just come back from the place.

JAN: You've just come back from the pub.

TOM: Is that what this is about? Going for a drink? Leaving you here?

JAN: No. Of course not.

TOM: I've said I'm sorry, Jan. I'll make it up to you tomorrow. Tonight. We can get the hell out of here right now as far as I'm concerned.

JAN: I'm just trying to understand.

TOM: Understand what?

JAN: If you've come all the way up here – but only talked to other police – how's that going to help?

> TOM *stares at her.*

TOM: Look, Jan, I want to explain something to you. My brief here is about this big. (*He makes a little square with thumbs and forefingers.*) OK? I'm not here to talk to witnesses, or take statements, or play 'Ten Guitars' with the locals. All that, anything which is going to open up the whole thing again, is none of my business. It's outside my brief. (JAN *looks at him.*) The Commissioner asked me to come here, making as little fuss as possible, to do one specific thing. That's all. And that's all I've done.

JAN: What specific thing?

TOM: You don't need to know that, Jan. It's donkey work. About exhibits.

JAN: Exhibits?

TOM: Where something was found. That's all.

JAN: The cartridge case.

TOM, *sighing*: Oh, Jesus.

JAN: It's about where the cartridge case was found. In the garden!

TOM: Slow down.

JAN, *pleased*: That's alright then.

> TOM *lifts his head to look at her.*

TOM: Alright?
JAN: Mmm. (*She heads for the jug.*) Did you want tea or coffee?
TOM: Coffee. No, tea. (JAN *busies herself.*) So that's alright then?
  I can do my job, just the particular thing I've been assigned
  to do.
JAN: Your brief.
TOM: And that's alright with you.
JAN: Mmm.
TOM: Well that's a bloody relief I can tell you.

> *He moves behind her, kisses her neck.*

Why don't we join the locals in retiring early?
JAN, *smiling*: What for?
TOM: Got to get up for milking.
JAN: We don't.
TOM: Speak for yourself. I've been known to rise up early in the
  morning.
JAN: I'm so proud of you, Tom.
TOM, *looking at her*: You've never said that to me before.
JAN: Of course I have.
TOM: Not like that. (*He hesitates.*) Why are you proud?
JAN, *turning to face him*: I'm proud of you for doing what's right.
  Making a difference. For being the one to sort it all out.
TOM: Why don't we take that cup of tea to bed?

> *As he breaks away from her heading for the door –*

JAN: I mean it's straightforward, isn't it? (TOM *stops and looks at
  her.*) The cartridge case.

> *Pause.*

Tom: And if I was to agree with you there, Jan, what exactly would I be agreeing to?

Jan: It couldn't have fallen where it was found.

Tom: As you were. Make mine a coffee.

Jan: If the bullet was fired through the louvre windows beside the back door then the cartridge case ejected, it couldn't have landed in a garden twenty feet away.

Tom: Who said it was twenty feet?

Jan: Whatever it was.

Tom: 'Whatever' is not good enough, Jan. 'Whatever' won't stand up in court.

Jan: How far is it then?

Tom: I've been there and it's not twenty feet.

Jan: Did you measure it?

Tom: I know what twenty feet is and it was nowhere near.

Jan: Whatever the measurement, it was too far wasn't it?

Tom: There's that 'whatever' again.

Jan: It was too far for a cartridge to be ejected from a gun.

Tom: Depends what the gun is.

Jan: But you know what kind of gun. You know from the bullets. A point two-two.

Tom: Gunsmith now? Ballistics expert too.

Jan: Are you saying everyone's got it wrong? It was a different kind of gun?

Tom: I'm just saying.

Jan: What?

Tom: I'm just saying! It's easy to move the goalposts isn't it!

Jan: But that was the case. The cartridge case. It came from Thomas's gun. The point two-two. That was how they connected everything to him. If it wasn't a point two-two then it couldn't have been his gun and the cartridge case doesn't mean anything.

Tom: Who's saying that? I'm not saying that.

Jan: I thought you were.

Tom: What?

Jan: Saying.

Tom: What?

Jan: Something.

Tom, *looking at her*: Well I wasn't.

Jan: How far is the garden from the back door?

Tom: Who's to say it was the back door?

Jan: What?

Tom: Who's to say he didn't pick up the cartridge then drop it in the garden on his way out.

Jan: Is the garden on the way out?

Tom: He could've thrown it. He could've picked it up, then thrown it so it landed over in the garden where it was found.

Jan: Why?

Tom: Why what?

Jan: Why would someone do that?

Tom: He's a murderer. He doesn't need a reason why. Why murder them in the first place?

Jan: What did you say about the back door?

Tom: What?

Jan: You said, 'Who's to say it was the back door?'

Tom: He might've shot through another window. Closer to the garden. There's a number of possible scenarios.

Jan: That was the police case. That he shot through the louvres.

Tom: No it wasn't.

Jan: That he pointed the rifle through the open louvres, and fired through the kitchen into the lounge.

Tom: That's not the police case.

Jan: That's what they said he did. In court. That's what it all relied on.

Tom: That's the prosecution case. Not the police case.

Jan: But the prosecution took it from the police investigation.

Tom: They can do whatever the hell they like. Doesn't mean the police agree with it.

JAN: What is the police case?

TOM: We like to keep our options open. (JAN *looks at him.*) The
main bloody point is, Thomas said he'd never been near
the place. He says that himself. Then what's a cartridge
case from his rifle doing right outside the house? You're
keen on the questions, Jan. There's one for you. (*He goes
to make the coffee.*) Think about it, Jan. We're not mind-
readers. You want law and order to depend on being able to
figure out exactly, precisely, how some bastard did whatever
he did?

> JAN *seizes the opportunity to covertly consult the book she
> pulls out from under the chair cushion.*

You want to see a whole case cave in just because we said
he took a step over there and it turns out it was this way?
(*There is no answer.*) Eh?

JAN, *freezing*: No.

TOM: No, of course not. You don't want to see killers walking
free because of a three-minute difference in a timing, a
couple of inches short in an estimated height, or an ejected
cartridge case rolls a few feet.

> With the help of the postcard bookmark JAN *pinpoints
> what she's looking for in the book.*

JAN: Sixteen.

TOM: Eh?

> JAN *stuffs the book back under the cushion and sits on it.*

JAN: Sixteen feet. (TOM *approaches suspiciously. She looks up
at him.*) From the flowerbed to the window. I've just
remembered. (TOM *quickly reaches under her, under the
cushion.*) Tom! What are you doing?

> *He pulls out the book and gazes at it. Pause.*

Tom: Well, that's just bloody marvellous. (*He holds it up.* Jan
   can't meet his eye.) Can make up your own mind, eh? Form
   your own opinion.

Jan: It's just a book.

Tom: Like the usual sort of book you read? *Forever Amber?*
   Penmarric?

   Jan *doesn't reply.*

   You know what this is? It's anti-police for one thing. It's
   sensationalist . . . garbage.

Jan: You haven't even read it.

Tom: I don't need to read it. The question is why the hell are you
   reading it? Where'd you get it from?

Jan: The library.

Tom, *checking the back of the book*: It's overdue. (*He snaps the
   book shut.*) Did someone put you up to this? One of those
   organisations? Retrial committee or something?

Jan: No.

Tom: Someone approach you?

Jan: No. Who?

Tom: Somebody at the kids' schools. A parent, or a teacher.

Jan: No.

Tom: Could be anybody. Somebody's cousin's wife. Connected
   down the line somehow. It's a small country, Jan – you've
   got to watch yourself.

Jan: Nobody talked to me. I was just interested.

Tom: Especially with the position I'm in now. HQ. People find
   out who you are, it makes sense they'll try to bend your ear,
   get to me through you.

Jan: Nobody's trying to get to anybody, Tom. I went to the
   library, I got the book because I was interested. And I'll pay
   the overdue fine.

   Jan *puts her hand out for the book.* Tom *doesn't give it to*
   her.

Tom: Interested. You're just interested.

Jan: Yes.

Tom: Why?

Jan: Why what?

Tom: Why now? Why this?

Jan: I don't know. I just got interested. I read about it in the paper. I started reading the articles.

Tom *hefts the book.*

Tom: How are you going to pay the library fine?

Jan: What?

Tom: The library fine. What are you going to pay it with?

Jan: It's only a few days. It can't be more than fifty cents.

Tom: Yeah, whose fifty cents? Where did that fifty cents come from? (Jan *just looks at him.*) It came from me, Jan. And where did I get it? From my employer. From the New Zealand Police Force. You understand me? (*There is no response.*) I'm getting paid to be a cop, and you're spending the money on something that holds us in contempt, that says we're just a bunch of dickheads. Or worse.

Jan: I'll give you the fifty cents back. I'll get my purse.

Tom, *grabbing her wrist*: That's not what I'm saying. You know it's not.

Jan: There's all those Fanta bottles out in the garage. I can take them back, get the deposit, use that to pay the library. That way I'll be a woman of independent means.

Tom: Have I ever begrudged you money, Jan? You're my wife, you're entitled. But you've got to pay some attention to where it's coming from. You, and me, we've got to know where we stand. Which side of the line.

Jan: What line?

Tom: Oh come on, Jan.

Jan: What line are you talking about?

Tom: Alright. The line between the people who take on the job

of upholding justice – and order – and other people who're
dead set on opposing that.

JAN: Criminals?

TOM: Some of them.

JAN: And others?

TOM: People who . . . can't resist sticking their nose in where they
shouldn't. Maybe some of them with the right motive, who
knows? The rest of them because they can't stand authority
of any sort. Simple as that. (*He brandishes the book.*) Take a
look at this lot. Born bloody stirrers.

JAN: And I'm to keep well away from them.

TOM: It's thanks to them that it's going to be the police on trial
this time round. You can't have your cake and eat it too,
Jan. You can't throw stones and live in the glasshouse.
(*Passionately*) Jesus, why can't you just once . . . ?

JAN: What?

TOM *looks at her then turns away.*

TOM: But that's you all over. Truth is it's bloody typical.

JAN: What's typical?

TOM: I don't talk about my work. Right? Don't bring it home
with me, leave it at the door. Why's that?

JAN: I told you. Because I was frightened for you and there was
nothing I could do.

TOM: Frightened for me?

JAN: Yes.

TOM: You could've fooled me. (*He sits across the room from her.*)
I'll tell you why I stopped talking about the job shall I?
Because in the early days, when I did, when I'd come home
and I'd be telling you about tackling some scrote with a
bloody fence batten or a knife. Wherever it was, on the
street, in someone's bloody kitchen, up some right-of-way
all on my lonesome. Taking some bastard down. Yeah?
And here I'd be at home telling you about it, and what
would you say? Eh?

JAN: I don't remember.

TOM: Like clockwork. Every time. You'd say, 'That's some mother's son. He was somebody's baby once.'

JAN, *confused*: But he was.

TOM: That 'somebody's baby' was trying to tear my head off! Cut my bloody heart out! And you – you'd take their side!

JAN: No.

TOM: I'm telling you, Jan. You were thinking about them!

JAN: I couldn't help it.

TOM: Did you ever think that the story could've turned out different? Only if it did, you wouldn't be hearing it from me. The very fact that I was sitting there telling it to you meant I'd come through. Every day, every night that I was out there, I never knew what was coming next. I was that scared, Jan. If one of those bastards had managed to stick me in the chest, there'd have been nothing there. Because my heart was up here the whole time. In my bloody mouth! (*He takes a breath.*)

And I come home to you, looking for some sort of . . . I dunno, understanding. And all you're worried about is their problems! I used to wonder, do the other guys have to put up with this? I'd ask them and, oh no, when they went home after a tussle their wives were ready to march down the cells and finish the bastards off. They knew where they stood.

JAN: I couldn't congratulate you for hurting somebody.

TOM: Not somebody. The right body. The bad guy! (JAN *doesn't reply.*) So I just – stopped telling you about it. Stopped talking. Kept conversation to the kids, what you did. You didn't seem to mind. It seemed to suit you.

JAN: I'm sorry.

TOM: Yeah, but that's you, Jan. And that's why you're typical. Because there's so many of you. You're happy to benefit from the job but you don't want to know how it's done. The dirty details. Until all of a sudden up goes the cry. Injustice! Some poor bugger, ex-choirboy most likely, banged up inside who just might not have done it after all. And that grabs your interest doesn't it? Not all the bad bastards we had to fight tooth and nail to get in there. Not the ones still on the street who'd be put away in five seconds flat if the courts played ball. No, you're much more interested in just the one time, the one case where you think we might have got it wrong. Because we're only out there up to our necks in it doing the job, whereas you, home in your armchair with your book, you just know better!

JAN: I don't know better. But there's all these questions.

TOM: There's always questions!

JAN: But so many.

TOM: Do you have any idea of the kind of painstaking detail that goes into an investigation like this? Do you honestly think that after all that time, all that sorting and examining every last little thing, that we're just going to go and get it all wrong? Or just break all the rules? Because that's what they're saying, isn't it? (*He taps the book.*) They're saying that cartridge case was planted.

JAN: They don't say by who.

TOM: It's obvious by who. You think if it was me – that I could do that? Plant evidence?

JAN: But it wasn't you. You've said yourself, some police are deadweight. The rest of you are carrying them. I've heard you saying it.

TOM: These are detectives, Jan. Senior detectives. This is serious stuff – a murder inquiry. We're all up to speed on it. If you're talking about them you're talking about me too. (JAN *looks at him.*)
    So come on, Jan. I want to know. Do you think I could do that? Do you think I'm that useless at my job? Is that what you think of me? Eh?

JAN, *quiet*: No. I know you wouldn't.

TOM: Right.

JAN: But someone did. They must've, Tom. It stands to reason.

TOM: A cop?

JAN: Someone who thought he was doing the right thing because he believed Thomas was guilty.

TOM: We're trained to be impartial, keep the personal out of it.

JAN: That garden was searched four times.

TOM: Not sieve-searched. They could've missed it.

JAN: You said they don't make mistakes.

TOM: We're human!

JAN: It doesn't make sense, Tom.

TOM: Would you and every other bloody busybody in the country mind leaving that to the jury?

JAN: Alright, never mind the cartridge case. What about everything else?

TOM: How many times, Jan? That's my brief – *only* the cartridge case.

JAN: But it's obvious that Thomas couldn't have left it there.

TOM: Obvious? Why the hell is it obvious?

JAN: Because he didn't kill them!

TOM: Eh?

JAN: Because I know who did – and it wasn't him!

> *Pause.*

TOM: You know who did it?

JAN, *nodding*: Mmm.

> TOM *looks at her a long moment.*

TOM: Good.

> *He clears the plates from the table.*

JAN: Don't you want to know who it was?

Tom: Why don't I just read it in the book for myself? (*He turns to go again.*)
Jan: It was her. She did it. She killed her husband.
Tom, *sighing*: Jesus, Mary and Joseph.
Jan: They were having an argument and he hit her. So she got the gun and shot him. It was about the curtains.
Tom: The what?
Jan: There were no curtains in the house.
Tom: Jan—
Jan: Twice she'd ordered curtains and both times he'd rung up and cancelled them.
Tom: You're saying she killed him because he wouldn't buy her curtains?
Jan: She had money from her inheritance but he wouldn't let her spend it. It always had to be the farm!
Tom: That's total speculation.
Jan: You can't live like that. You can't make a home without curtains.
Tom: You have to make some sacrifices. He was just a working joker trying to get along.
Jan: He broke her jaw.
Tom: You don't know that!
Jan: She killed him – then days later she killed herself.
Tom: The murder–suicide theory.
Jan: She was the woman standing at the gate – two days after her husband was last seen – two days after she shot him.
Tom: If there was a woman seen round that house, and I mean if, it could have been anyone, the description was so vague.
Jan: It was her.
Tom: According to who?
Jan: The fold on the nappy.
Tom: Eh?
Jan: The nappy on the baby couldn't have been more than a couple of days old. It was folded in a special nurse's fold. And she'd been a nurse!

Tom: I don't believe this.

Jan: She put that nappy on the baby. There was no mystery woman.

Tom: Curtains. And nappies.

Jan: She was going mad with the pain. She couldn't go to the doctor. She couldn't think straight, she couldn't even get the blood out of the carpet.

Tom: And after she put a bullet in her head – what? She wrapped herself up, put herself in the river? (*He looks at her.*) Don't tell me – you think her father did that.

Jan: He'd already helped her get rid of the husband's body. After she killed herself he thought it would all get blamed on him.

Tom: But instead we blamed it on someone else. Is that it? End of storytime?

Jan: It's the simplest explanation. It fits, Tom.

Tom: Oh, it fits alright, Jan. It fits my arse. And I'm not even going to tell you how far it is from the facts. Because you know what? I've had enough of this. I'm going to bed.

Jan: Tom, this is important! If he didn't do it, the cartridge case was planted –

Tom, *waving her off*: Forget it, Jan.

Jan: – and there's an innocent man in prison!

Tom, *stopping and whirling back to her*: I'll tell you what kind of 'innocent man' we're talking about! This is someone who'll leave a baby to starve to death in her crib!

Jan: No –

Tom: I've been up there, Jan. That place is back from the road, off by itself, there's no way anyone's going to hear a kid crying in that house. Crying for bloody days, Jan. Days on end! That could have been Clare or Bevan at that age! You and me slaughtered in our own home, and this bastard just walks out leaving our baby all alone to die! That's your innocent man! That's who you want to let out on the street!

That's who you'd rather stand behind than me! Your own bloody husband!

JAN *stares at him, pale and shaken.*

JAN: You think he did it.

TOM *can't meet her eye.*

(*Slowly.*) You've convinced yourself he's guilty. That's what you're going to say.

TOM: It's not up to me to say anything about him.

JAN: You'll say the cartridge case could have fallen there. You'll say that because you believe he's guilty.

TOM: What I believe has got nothing to do with it.

JAN: I thought you were going to free him. I thought that's what we'd come here for.

TOM: Jan, I'm whacked. Maybe I did have one over the odds at the pub.

JAN: I thought you'd do the right thing. I knew you would. I've been sitting here all day.

TOM: Let's just sleep on it, eh?

JAN: Tom, you can't.

TOM: For God's sake, give it a rest, Jan.

JAN: You can't tell them it's alright when it's not.

TOM: Now you're going too far.

JAN: When someone put it there. When it was planted!

TOM: That's enough!

JAN: You can't say that!

TOM *snatches up the book.*

TOM: This bloody book!

JAN: You can't help them keep him locked up. When he didn't do it!

TOM: I'm not helping anyone do anything! I'm doing my job!

This is my work! You understand? And no one, including you, is going to tell me how to do it.

He jerks open a top cupboard and tosses the book inside, slamming the cupboard door.

And I don't want to hear another bloody word about it!

JAN sinks into a chair, her image of TOM – and with it her whole world – rocked. She starts to sob noiselessly.

TOM paces the room like a fish hooked to JAN's crying. When he can't stand it any more he goes to her.

Jesus, Jan. (*JAN doesn't look at him.*) Come on. (*He puts his arm around her.*) Look, we got a bit carried away, eh?

JAN: I'm frightened, Tom.

TOM: Let's have a cup of tea, and a night's sleep, and get the hell out of here in the morning. You'll feel better. God, I know I will.

JAN, *looking at him*: Tom, I'm frightened.

TOM: Frightened of what? Eh? (*She just stares at him.*)
     For God's sake, Jan. You know me. You know me better than anyone. You don't seriously think I'd get involved in anything? That I'd be part of a cover-up? (*JAN doesn't reply.*) I would never ever do anything like that. (*TOM stares at her, also rocked to his core.*)
     Jan – look – I need you to trust me. You're my wife for Pete's sake. I need you to trust that whatever I say, it's the right thing. It's as right as I can make it.

JAN: I want to trust you, Tom.

TOM: You can't be measuring me up every five minutes. Checking me against some ruler to see how right I am.

JAN: But this is somebody's life.

TOM: Too right! Our life!

He takes a breath. He holds her hand in his.

There's got to be faith. That I'm doing my best. What kind of marriage is it otherwise?

JAN: I want to.

TOM: Otherwise what's the point? There's no point is there?

JAN: I want to have faith in you, Tom.

They stare at each other.

TOM: Then do. Just – leave it up to me. Forget all the questions. Just trust me.

JAN: And it'll be alright?

TOM: We'll be alright.

She stares at him, seeking his reassurance. Slowly she nods.

Yeah? (JAN *nods again.*) That's my girl.

He embraces her, holds her close. PHILLIP *appears outside the open louvres holding a rifle. He's just closing the bolt.* TOM *looks up at the sound and sees* PHILLIP.

What the hell!

PHILLIP *ducks out of sight.*

Get down!

JAN: What?

TOM: Down!

He grabs JAN *and throws her behind cover. Yanking open the door he rushes out. Confused,* JAN *half rises.*

JAN: Tom?

There's a shout from outside, the sound of a scuffle. TOM *bursts back in, dragging* PHILLIP *in a crushing headlock.* TOM *holds the rifle in his other hand.*

Tom, *adrenaline charged*: What the hell are you doing with this? Eh?

Phillip: Nothing!

> Tom *drops the rifle on the chair and shoves* Phillip *up against the wall, twisting his arm painfully up his back. The picture on the wall is knocked off kilter.*

Tom: What are you after? Sneaking round.

Jan: Tom, no, you're hurting him.

Tom: Some sort of perv. Is that what you are?

Jan: Let him go, Tom.

Tom: You know what you get for pointing a gun at a cop?

Phillip: I didn't.

Tom: I saw you!

Phillip: She asked me to bring it.

Tom, *still to* Phillip: You got something to tell me? Eh?

Jan: It's true.

> Jan *picks up the rifle.*

Tom: Like pointing rifles through windows, do you?

> Phillip *is hurt, sobbing.*

Jan: I asked him to show me.

Tom: What do you know about the shootings?

Phillip: What shootings?

Tom: The Crewes! What do you know about the Crewes?

Phillip: Nothing!

Jan: He hasn't done anything!

> Tom *feels something under* Phillip's *shirt.*

Tom: What the bloody hell?

> *He pulls* Phillip's *shirt open –*

PHILLIP: No!

> *– yanking it down over his shoulders.* TOM *stares.*

TOM: Jesus.

> PHILLIP *is wearing one of his mother's bras. He tries to slump but* TOM *holds him up, his arms trapped in his shirt, so he can't cover himself.*

You are a bloody pervo.

> PHILLIP *sobs.*

JAN: Tom. Let him go.
TOM: I'm taking you down to the local cop right now.
PHILLIP: No! No, please!
TOM: We'll get to the bottom of this if I have to parade you through the public bar.

> PHILLIP *struggles violently as* TOM *pushes him towards the door.*

PHILLIP: Please!
JAN: You're hurting him!
TOM: He tried to shoot us!
JAN: He didn't!

> PHILLIP *buckles, collapsing to the floor.*

TOM: Cut that out! (TOM *hoists* PHILLIP.) Get up and walk! Walk!
JAN, *unable to stand it*: Listen to me! Listen to me!

> TOM *finally flicks a glance in her direction.*

TOM: Put that down!
JAN: I asked him to bring it! I asked him to show me!
TOM: Put it down, Jan!

JAN: He was only trying to show me! The – the thingy!

Distraught, she works the lever, trying to demonstrate.

TOM: Yeah, alright Jan.
JAN: I just wanted to see if it was sixteen feet!
TOM: Jan. (TOM *has his hand out, is moving towards her.*)
JAN, *working the bolt*: To see! That's all!

> JAN *slams home the bolt. The rifle fires, the report huge in the confined space. There's a moment of absolute dead stillness, the three of them in a frozen tableau.*

TOM, *softly, eyes closed*: Jesus, Mary and Joseph.

> PHILLIP *takes a huge sobbing breath, and pitches forward onto the floor. He clutches his shattered shin, blood leaking out onto the carpet. Stunned,* JAN *and* TOM *watch him.*

JAN: There's blood. He's bleeding.

> TOM *returns his attention to her.*

TOM: Give me the gun, Jan.

> JAN *seems spellbound, watching* PHILLIP.

Just give me the gun.

> *He reaches out and takes it from her. This seems to wake her up.*

JAN: Tom, call an ambulance. Call an ambulance, Tom!
PHILLIP: No! I'm alright!
JAN: You're bleeding. You have to go to the hospital.
PHILLIP: No!

> *He tries to pull his tattered shirt round himself.* JAN *goes to him.*

JAN: Stay still.

TOM: Don't move, don't touch anything. I'm in charge here.

JAN: Tom – the phone.

> TOM *crosses to the phone, but sinks into a chair beside it.*

PHILLIP, *sobbing*: I don't want anyone to see me.

JAN: We can take it off.

> *She moves to touch the bra, but* PHILLIP *flinches away.*

PHILLIP: You'll tell!

JAN: We won't. We won't, will we Tom?

> *She looks up, sees* TOM *is staring at her.*

TOM: What the hell have you done, Jan? How am I supposed to straighten this out?

JAN: It was an accident.

TOM: There'll have to be an inquiry. You'll get dragged through it. What about the kids? The new job? Christ, HQ doesn't even know you're here. They told me to come up here on the quiet! (*He looks at her.*) It's all fucked, Jan. Everything we've worked for.

> *Seeing his chance,* PHILLIP *grabs* JAN's *arm.*

PHILLIP: You go.

JAN: What?

PHILLIP: I'll be alright by myself.

JAN: But you've been shot.

> PHILLIP *looks between* JAN *and* TOM.

PHILLIP: I did it myself. While I was cleaning the gun. It was an accident.

JAN: But it was an accident.

PHILLIP, *pleading*: I won't say anything. Ever. I promise. If you just go.

> TOM *is now staring at* PHILLIP.

JAN: Tom?

> TOM *doesn't respond.*

PHILLIP: I don't want you here.
JAN: We can't just leave. (JAN *looks to* TOM.) Tom?

> TOM *still seems oblivious.* JAN *crosses to the phone, but* TOM *puts his hand on it to stop her calling. They gaze at each other for a long moment.*

TOM: Get your stuff.

> JAN *stares at him in disbelief.*

Do what I say! Get your stuff.

> *Frightened and confused,* JAN *backs away.*

PHILLIP, *rocking*: I'm alright. I'm alright.

> JAN *moves to the door of the bedroom and hesitates. She watches as* TOM, *still holding the rifle, crosses to* PHILLIP. *He pulls the bolt back, ejecting the cartridge case. He checks the rifle is empty, and hands it to* PHILLIP. TOM *looks up to see* JAN *staring at him. They hold each other's gaze.*

> *The sound of the cartridge case being ejected is heard again, echoed and magnified many times until it fills the space, as music ('Do It Again' by Steely Dan) comes in and the lights go down to black.*

> *The End.*